Japan's Contribution to the World

装幀 ● 菊地信義

装画 ● 野村俊夫

編者 ● 外務省大臣官房海外広報課

翻訳 ● William R. Carter

DTP・図版 ● 山下恭弘

編集 ● 翻訳情報センター

Published by Kodansha International Ltd.,
17-14, Otowa 1-chome, Bunkyo-ku, Tokyo 112–8652.

First Edition 1999

ISBN4-7700-2192-5
99 00 10 9 8 7 6 5 4 3 2 1

国際貢献Q&A
世界で活躍する日本人
Japan's Contribution to the World

外務省大臣官房海外広報課 編

はじめに

　現在、国際化と国境を越えた人的交流の進展に伴い、外国人の対日理解において、日本人との接触の経験が果たす重要性が日に日に高まっております。今や、読者の皆様一人一人が、国際社会の情報発信の重要な担い手であるといっても過言ではありません。

　しかしながら、読者の皆様の多くが常々感じられておられるかとは思いますが、外国人から日本のことを色々質問されたときに、基本的な情報の無いまま、とっさに英語で説明するのは難しいと思います。このような場合、簡単な言葉でわかりやすく日本について説明した参考書の類があれば、大変有益ではないかと思います。

　本書では「国際貢献」をテーマとし、以上のような読者の方々の使いやすさを考えて、日英対訳のQ&A形式に編集してみました。国際貢献を取り上げたのは、国際社会での日本の重要度が益々増加している今日、国際社会での日本の「貢献」のあり方が、国内外の高い関心事項となっているからです。しかしながらその一方で、日本の国際貢献のあり方に対し、「日本は金だけ出して人を出さない」とか、「日本の貢献にはポリシーがない」という非難がしばしば聞かれます。これは、日本の国際貢献のあり方を見て、外国の人達はそこに人と人とのつながりが見られないと感じているからではないでしょうか。

　実際には多くの日本人の方が広範な分野で国

FOREWORD

With the progress of globalization and interpersonal contacts that transcend national borders, foreigners' direct experiences of personal contacts with Japanese are recently becoming more important day by day as one of the elements of their understanding of Japan. It is not too much to say that each of your readers can play an important role in giving information about Japan to international society.

Most of us, however, may have the same feeling that it is difficult, when we are asked various questions about Japan by people from other countries, to respond promptly in English, especially if we lack basic information. So I think concise and easily understandable reference books can be very useful in explaining things about Japan in simple language.

This book, which focuses on "international contributions," has been edited in a Q&A style, in both Japanese and English, in the hope that it will be easy to use. The reason why "international contribution" was chosen as the book's theme is that, as a result of Japan's growing importance in the international community, Japan's contribution to it is of growing interest both in Japan and in other countries. We often hear criticism like "Japan provides money but not people" or "Japan's international contributions lack a comprehensive principle." Perhaps one reason for such criticism is that foreigners may feel it is hard to see the human ties between individuals which are a part of this contribution.

In fact, a large number of Japanese are working hard

際社会のために真摯に働いておられます。ただ、このような事実は今まで余りスポットを当てられておらず、日本でも案外知られていないようです。

　そこで本書では、日本の「国際貢献」を俯瞰するとともに、国際社会のために働く日本人の方々を取り上げ、これら一人一人の方の草の根レベルでの取り組みを紹介することに努めました。

　読者の皆様が、本書を読まれることによって、日本の「国際貢献」のあり方に対する理解がより一層深められ、また、何かの折に外国人に日本の「国際貢献」について説明する際に、本書で得た知識を有効に活用されることがあれば、これに勝る喜びはありません。

　最後に、本書制作にあたり、講談社インターナショナルおよび翻訳情報センターのスタッフの方々、翻訳者ウイリアム・R・カーター氏には大変お世話になりました。謹んでお礼申し上げます。

外務省大臣官房海外広報課長　新美　潤

for the benefit of international society in a wide range of fields. These realities have not, up to now, been adequately paid attention to by the public and still go largely unnoticed, even in Japan.

This book, which gives an overall picture of Japan's "international contribution," introduces several individual Japanese and describes how they are engaged in beneficial activities at the "grassroots level" in various parts of the world.

I will certainly feel very happy if, by reading this book, you gain a deeper understanding of Japan's "international contributions" and are furthermore able to utilize effectively some of the knowledge gained from this book when on some future occasion you will be explaining something about Japan's "international contributions" to people from other countries.

I wish to express my sincere gratitude to the staff members of Kodansha International and Translation Services Inc., and to the translator, William R. Carter, who helped to produce this valuable book.

Niimi Jun
   Director of the Overseas Public Relations Division,
   Ministry of Foreign Affairs

◆目次◆

国際貢献 Q&A

世界で活躍する日本人
Japan's Contribution to the World

世界平和の
ために
For Peace
in the World

Chapter

Q 世界のどこで、どのような紛争が
起こっているのですか。

第2次世界大戦が終わってから続いてきた
東側陣営と西側陣営との間の冷戦は、1989
年のベルリンの壁の崩壊、1991年のソ連の
解体で終わりを告げました。

しかし、その後の世界では、旧ソ連やバ
ルカン諸国のように、冷戦時代には社会主
義勢力の支配の中で押さえつけられていた
民族間の抗争が再燃したり、アフガニスタ
ンのように、1989年のソ連軍の撤退後、力
の真空が生じたのを契機に新たな勢力間の
紛争に突入したりといった地域もあります。
また、私たちの日本に近い朝鮮半島では、

A Japanese NGO staff worker helping refugees ▲

Q Where do conflicts in the world occur,
   and what kinds of disputes are they?

The Cold War, which continued between "Eastern"
and "Western" camps following the Second World War,
came to an end with the fall of the Berlin Wall in 1989 and
the dissolution of the Soviet Union in 1991.

Afterwards, however, in various parts of the world,
such as in the former Soviet Union and the Balkan Peninsula,
disputes flared up again between ethnic groups that during the
Cold War had been kept in check by socialist regimes. As
well as this, regions in which there was a "power vacuum,"
such as Afghanistan after the withdrawal of Soviet troops in
1989, were plunged into new armed conflicts between mutually antagonistic political forces. On the Korean Peninsula,

冷戦時代の対立構造が残っており緊張が続いています。

その一方、冷戦時代には東西両陣営の対立の焦点となっていたグアテマラ、エルサルバドル、中東さらにはアンゴラなど一部のアフリカ地域等で、冷戦終結後に和平が成立してきています。その中には米国が主導的役割を果たした中東和平の例もありますが、グアテマラ、エルサルバドルのように、国際的枠組みの中での国際紛争の解決のために国連が主導的役割を果たしてきている例もあります。そしてこれら和平の実現・定着に日本

冷戦終結後の世界の地域紛争
Regional Conflicts in the Post-Cold War World

which is very near Japan, the divided political structure of the Cold War era remains, and tensions continue unresolved.

On the other hand, in regions such as Guatemala, El Salvador, the Middle East, Angola and other parts of Africa that had been a focus of confrontation between Eastern and Western camps during the Cold War, the end of this period is bringing about peace. In some cases, such as the Middle East Peace Process, the United States has played a leading role, and in other cases, such as Guatemala and El Salvador, the United Nations has played the leading role in resolving disputes within an international framework. Japan, too, has been cooperating in various ways to realize these peace objec-

❶ エクアドル✕ペルー Ecuador vs. Peru
1995年、豊富な天然資源があるコンドル山脈地帯の国境において武力衝突。
Armed conflict in 1995 over borders in the resources-rich Sierra del Condor region.

❷ パキスタン✕インド Pakistan vs. India
カシミールの帰属をめぐって、国境において武力衝突が続く。
Continuing border conflicts, motivated by the status of Kashmir.

**❸ サウジアラビア✕イエメン
Saudi Arabia vs. Yemen**
国境をめぐって、1994年から翌年にかけて武力衝突。
Armed conflicts over borders in 1994 and 1995.

❹ イラク✕クウェート Iraq vs. Kuwait
1990年、イラク軍による侵攻。多国籍軍が加わって、翌年、クウェートを解放。
In response to the 1990 Iraqi invasion of Kuwait, a multinational force liberates Kuwait the following year.

**❺ カメルーン✕ナイジェリア
Cameroon vs. Nigeria**
油田地帯である半島の領有権をめぐって、1996年に武力衝突。
Armed conflict in 1996 over ownership of an oil-producing peninsula.

**❻ モーリタニア✕セネガル
Mauritania vs. Senegal**
国境をめぐって、武力衝突を繰り返している。
Repeated armed conflicts over borders.

も様々な形で協力してきています。

 Q 核軍縮のために日本はどのような
努力をしているのですか。

　冷戦時代の核軍拡競争により、現在、地球上には全人類を何十回も抹殺しうるほどの数の核兵器が存在しています。この核兵器を無くしていくことは、広島・長崎の被爆体験を持つ私たち日本だけでなく、国際社会全体の願いです。

　この願いをどう実現していくかについて、核兵器保有国に対して、即時、あるいは期限を付けて核廃絶を約束させるための条約締結の交渉を、直ちに開始すべきという主張があります。しかし、日本としては、核兵器保有国の核軍縮交渉への参加を得ながら、核軍縮措置を一歩一歩積み上げていくことが現実的でありまた核兵器のない世界を実現するために実はもっとも早い方法であると考えています。こうした考え方に基づき日本が提出した「核兵器の究極的な廃絶に向けた核軍縮に関する決議」は、1994年、国連総会で圧倒的多数の賛成を得て採択されています。

　また、日本は核保有国の増加防止のために、核不拡散条約(NPT)の無期限延長、核兵器の質的向上に歯止めをかけるなどの包括的核実験禁止条約(CTBT)の締結に努力してきました。さらに、日本は次の目標として、核兵器の原料となる核分裂性物質の生産を禁止するカットオフ条約❖1 の締結交渉を早期に開始することを提案しています。

tives and help them to take root.

Q What sorts of efforts is Japan making for nuclear disarmament?

As a result of the nuclear arms race of the Cold War era, the number of nuclear weapons that exist in today's world is enough to destroy all of mankind dozens of times over. Eliminating these weapons is the fervent wish not only of Japan, which experienced the nuclear bombings of Hiroshima and Nagasaki, but of international society as a whole.

As for how to realize this wish, one point of view is that negotiations should be begun immediately to complete treaties that would have the nuclear weapons-possessing states promise to eliminate these weapons either immediately or within a time-bound framework. The Japanese government believes the most realistic and fastest means of realizing a nuclear weapons-free world is to build up nuclear disarmament measures step by step, while at the same time participating in nuclear disarmament negotiations among the nuclear weapons-possessing states. In 1994, Japan submitted to the UN General Assembly a "Resolution on Nuclear Disarmament with a View to the Ultimate Elimination of Nuclear Weapons," which was based on this sort of approach and was adopted by the General Assembly by an overwhelming majority of votes.

Japan made concerted efforts for the indefinite extension of the Nuclear Nonproliferation Treaty (NPT), which seeks to prevent the appearance of additional countries possessing nuclear weaponry, and also for the conclusion of the Comprehensive Nuclear Test Ban Treaty (CTBT), which seeks to apply a brake to the qualitative advancement of nuclear weaponry. As a further goal, Japan advocates the early conclusion of negotiations for a fissile material cut-off

その他にも、旧ソ連の核兵器解体を支援するために、ロシア、ウクライナ、カザフスタン、ベラルーシとそれぞれ2国間の協定を結び、核弾頭の解体から生じる核物質の貯蔵施設への協力、液体放射性廃棄物処理施設の建設、カザフスタンにある旧ソ連の核実験場の汚染対策、被爆者への医療支援などを進めています。

注1 "カットオフ"とは、核兵器およびその他の核爆発装置用のプルトニウムおよび高濃縮ウランの生産禁止のことで、CTBTに続く多国間の核軍縮・核不拡散措置の審議のため、98年8月、ジュネーブ軍縮会議(CD)においてカットオフ特別委員会の設置が決定された。

Q 核兵器の廃絶の問題以外に、世界の軍縮にとってはどのような問題がありますか。

米ソ両国の対立が終わり、冷戦の時代に真剣に恐れられていた大規模な核戦争の勃発の危険性は減少してきました。しかし、現在でも国際社会では実際に、民族、宗教、歴史上の経緯に起因する対立や、経済的利益の対立のために紛争が起こっています。

核兵器と並ぶ大量破壊兵器である化学兵

treaty ❖1 to prohibit the production of fissile materials for nuclear weapons.

Japan has concluded bilateral agreements with Russia, Ukraine, Kazakstan and Belarus, with a view to providing assistance for dismantling nuclear weapons of the former Soviet Union. Under these agreements Japan is helping build facilities to store nuclear materials derived from the dismantlement of nuclear warheads, is building facilities to dispose of liquid radioactive wastes, is helping alleviate the environmental damage caused by the former Soviet Union's nuclear tests in Kazakstan, and is providing medical assistance for persons affected by these tests.

NOTE 1 "Cut-off" refers to prohibiting the production of plutonium and highly enriched uranium for explosive devices. In August 1998, it was decided to establish within the Conference on Disarmament (CD) in Geneva a special committee for multilateral deliberation on further measures, following the CTBT, for nuclear disarmament and nonproliferation, such as a fissile materials cut-off treaty.

Q In addition to the elimination of nuclear weapons, what are some of the other global disarmament issues?

With the end of the confrontation between the United States and the Soviet Union, the danger of the outbreak of a large-scale nuclear war—a serious threat during the Cold War era—has lessened. However, disputes in international society still in fact continue to arise because of differences in economic interests or differences growing out of historical, religious or ethnic circumstances.

Chemical and biological weapons, which, like nuclear

器や生物兵器の存在も、世界の平和と安定を阻害するものですが、これに対しては、日本や他の国々の努力により禁止条約が結ばれてきました。さらに、大量破壊兵器の運搬手段であるミサイルの拡散を防ぐために国際的な輸出管理体制としてMTCR(ミサイル輸出管理レジーム)❖2 があります。

また、通常兵器に関する取り組みも重要です。日本がEC諸国(現在はEU諸国)と共同で提案した国連軍備登録制度は、各国の兵器輸出入に関するデータを自発的に国連に提出させることにより、軍備の透明性を高め、兵器の過度の蓄積を防止することを意図しており、各国がお互いへの信頼を深め合うことに役立っています。さらにはいわゆる通常兵器に関しては、その過剰な移転と蓄積の防止のために、冷戦時代のココム(対共産圏輸出統制委員会)の代わりとなるワッセナー・アレンジメント❖3が1996年に発足しています。

さらに日本政府は対人地雷の規制・禁止について、特定通常兵器使用禁止・制限条約の強化された地雷等に関する議定書の条約加盟国となる(97年6月)とともに、1997年12月、対人地雷禁止条約にも署名しました。

注2 日、米、欧州諸国、ロ、南アなど参加32ヵ国による、ミサイル本体および関連資機材・技術の輸出管理のための体制。たとえば、搭載可能重量500kg以上、射程300km以上のミサイル、ロケット等

weapons, are weapons of mass destruction, also threaten world peace and stability, and treaties to prohibit them have been realized through the efforts of Japan and other countries. To prevent the spread of missiles which can be used to deliver weapons of mass destruction, there is an international export control regime known as the MTCR (Missile Technology Control Regime)❖2.

Dealing with conventional weapons is also very important. The United Nations Register of Conventional Arms, which was put forward jointly by Japan and the European Community (EC, now European Union or EU) countries, is designed to improve the transparency of armaments and prevent the excessive accumulation of weapons by having each country voluntarily submit to the United Nations data on its arms trade. The register is playing a role in helping countries enhance mutual trust. To prevent the excessive transfer or accumulation of so-called conventional weapons, there is the Wassenaar Arrangement ❖3, which was established in 1996, replacing the Cold War-era COCOM (Coordinating Committee for Export to Communist Areas).

Japan is one of the countries subscribing to the protocol (concluded in June 1997) which strengthened the provisions with respect to anti-personnel landmines in the Convention on the Prohibitions or Restrictions on the Use of Certain Conventional Weapons Which May Be Deemed to Be Excessively Injurious or to Have Indiscriminate Effects. The Japanese government also signed the Anti-Personnel Landmines Ban Treaty, in December 1997.

NOTE 2   This is a system for controlling the export of missiles and related equipment and technology. It is participated in by 32 countries, including Japan, the United States, European countries, Russia, and South Africa. For example, it prohibits, in principle, the transfer of missiles, rockets, etc., capable of

は原則禁輸など。

注3　通常兵器および汎用品・技術の輸
出管理のための体制。日、米、欧州諸国、
ロ等33ヵ国が現在参加。

 世界ではテロに対して、
どのように取り組んでいますか。

　テロと言われる事件としては、1972年の
ミュンヘン五輪でパレスチナ・ゲリラがイス
ラエル選手団を襲撃した事件、88年のパン
ナム103号機爆破事件、95年の米オクラホ
マ連邦ビル爆破事件、様々な飛行機ハイジ
ャック事件など、様々なテロ事件のほか、
95年3月の東京地下鉄サリン事件や、96年
12月のペルー・リマの日本大使公邸占拠事
件、および97年11月のエジプトのルクソー
ルにおける観光客襲撃事件のように、私たち
に大きな衝撃を与えたものもあります。
　テロ防止に関しては、航空機の不法な奪
取の防止に関する条約、人質を取る行為に
関する国際条約、核物質の防護に関する条
約、海上航行の安全に対する不法な行為の
防止に関する条約など、11の関連条約が結
ばれてきています。

　さらに、1997年の米国デンバーでの主要国
首脳会議のコミュニケは「我々は、その動機の
いかんにかかわらずあらゆる形態のテロリズ
ムと闘う決意を再確認する。我々はテロリス
トの要求に譲歩することに反対し、……」と述

delivering at least a 500kg payload within a range of at least 300km.

NOTE 3 This regime controls the export of conventional arms and multi-use goods and technologies. It is participated in by 33 countries, including Japan, the United States, European countries, and Russia.

Q What kinds of measures are being taken against terrorism in the world?

Examples of terrorist incidents include the attack by Palestinian guerrillas on an Israeli team at the 1972 Olympic Games in Munich, the blowing up of Pan-Am flight #103 in 1988, the bombing of the United States Federal Building in Oklahoma City in 1995, and various cases of aircraft hijacking. Some terrorist attacks have had a particularly strong impact on the Japanese people, such as the March 1995 incident of toxic sarin gas released in a Tokyo subway, the seizure of the Japanese ambassador's residence in Lima, Peru, in December 1996, and the attack on tourists in Luxor, Egypt, in November 1997.

Eleven international conventions have been signed for the purpose of preventing terrorist activities. These include the Convention for the Suppression of Unlawful Seizure of Aircraft; the International Convention against the Taking of Hostages; the Convention on the Physical Protection of Nuclear Materials; and the Convention for the Suppression of Unlawful Acts against the Safety of Maritime Navigation.

The communiqué issued at the 1997 G-8 Summit in Denver asked all countries to join the above-mentioned international conventions on terrorism, stating: "We reconfirm our determination to combat terrorism in all forms, irrespective of motive. We oppose concessions to terrorist

べ、すべての国に対し2000年までに、上記の
テロに関する諸国際条約の締結国になるよう
呼びかけました。また首脳会議参加国は、国
連における爆弾テロ防止条約案に関する交渉
を主導しました。

さらに、時代の進展と共に、テロリストに
よるコンピューター・システムへの攻撃、テ
ロおよび犯罪目的のコンピューター・ネット
ワークの使用も切実な問題となってきてお
り、主要国首脳会議でも8ヵ国の首脳がその
防止のため情報、および手法を共有していく
ことを確認しました。

Q 国連は世界の平和にどのような役割を果たしているのですか。

国連は国際の平和と安全を維持すること
をその目的の1つとしており、そのための主
要な責任を果たす機関として安全保障理事
会があります。安保理は、拒否権を持つ米露
中英仏の5常任理事国を含む15の国で構成
されており、紛争の平和的解決のための勧
告、平和と安全の維持と回復のための勧告、
武力紛争やその他の重大問題の処理のため
の国際的な介入のための非軍事的あるいは軍
事的強制措置の決定等の任務を担っていま
す。

しかしながら、冷戦時代は米ソの激しい対
立と拒否権の行使のため、安保理は国際の
平和と安全の維持について当初予定されて
いた機能を十分に果たすことはできず、紛争
に際しては、国連がその中立性を生かして停

demands...." The G-8 Summit participants played a leading role in negotiations at the United Nations for the International Convention for the Suppression of Terrorist Bombings.

With the technological developments of our times, possible attacks on computer systems by terrorists, as well as the possible use of computer networks for terrorist or criminal purposes, have become problems of pressing relevance. The leaders of the eight countries represented at the G-8 Summit have confirmed their intention to share information and methods for the purpose of preventing such activities.

Q What sorts of roles does the United Nations play in support of world peace?

One of the goals of the United Nations is the maintenance of international peace and security. The main organ for fulfilling this responsibility is the United Nations Security Council, which is composed of 15 countries, including five permanent members (the United States, Russia, China, the United Kingdom, and France), which possess the right to veto Security Council decisions. The Security Council is responsible for making recommendations on the peaceful settlement of disputes, on the maintenance and/or restoration of peace and security, and decisions on imposing nonmilitary and military measures for international intervention to deal with armed conflicts and other serious matters.

During the Cold War era, due to serious confrontations between the United States and the Soviet Union and their exercise of veto rights, the Security Council was unable to fully exercise the functions originally intended for it in the field of maintaining international peace and security. Yet, in cases of

戦監視等を行う平和維持活動(Peacekeeping Operations: PKO)を行ってきました。

　冷戦の終結後、5常任理事国による拒否権の発動が際立って減り、安保理における意思決定が容易になりました。安保理の決定により派遣されるPKOの数が激増したことに加え、1990年の湾岸危機では安保理は、多国籍軍に対し武力の行使を行う権限を与える決議を採択するなど、非常に活発に機能しています。

展開中の国連平和維持活動
Current UN Peacekeeping Operations

armed conflicts, the United Nations has been using to advantage its position of neutrality in carrying out such Peacekeeping Operations (PKO) as the monitoring of cease-fire agreements.

After the end of the Cold War, the cases in which one or another of the five permanent members of the Security Council have exercised veto power have very noticeably decreased, and thus the making of decisions by the Council has been made easier. The number of Peacekeeping Operations dispatched in response to Security Council decisions has greatly increased and, in cases like the 1990 Persian Gulf Crisis, the Security Council has functioned in a very active way, adopting, for example, resolutions authorizing multinational troops to use military force.

❶国連プレブラカ監視団（UNMOP）
UN Mission of Observers in Prevlaka
国連東スラボニア暫定統治機関（UNTAES）
UN Transitional Authority in Eastern Slavonia
国連ボスニア・ヘルツェゴビナ・ミッション（UNMIBH）
UN Mission in Bosnia and Herzegovina
国連予防展開隊（UNPREDEP）
UN Preventive Deployment Force
❷国連西サハラ住民投票監視団（MINURSO）
UN Mission for the Referendum in Western Sahara
❸国連ハイチ暫定ミッション（UNTMIH）
UN Transitional Mission in Haiti
❹国連リベリア監視団（UNOMIL）
UN Observer Mission in Liberia
❺国連第3次アンゴラ検証団（UNAVEM III）
UN Angola Verification Mission III
❻キプロス国連平和維持軍（UNFICYP）
UN Peacekeeping Force in Cyprus
❼レバノン国連暫定軍（UNIFIL）
UN Interim Force in Lebanon
❽国連兵力引き離し監視軍（UNDOF）
UN Disengagement Observer Force
❾国連グルジア監視団（UNOMIG）
UN Observer Mission in Georgia
❿国連タジキスタン監視団（UNMOT）
UN Observer Mission in Tajikistan
⓫国連インド・パキスタン軍事監視団（UNMOGIP）
UN Military Observer Group in India and Pakistan
⓬国連イラク・クウェート監視団（UNIKOM）
UN Iraq-Kuwait Observation Mission
⓭パレスチナ国連停戦監視機構（UNTSO）
UN Truce Supervision Organization

さらに近年では、侵略や紛争への対処といった問題だけでなく、紛争によって生じる人権問題、難民問題や環境問題についても議論しています。

しかし安保理の行動も、新たにグローバルな役割を果たす意思と能力のある国が参加しなければ、真に正統かつ実効的な行動は起こせません。また、加盟国の増大をも踏まえ、議席を増やす必要性が指摘されています。

Q 国連平和維持活動は世界で どんな活躍をしていますか。

国連の平和維持活動(Peacekeeping Operations: PKO)は、国連が、国連加盟国から提供される人員からなる平和維持軍や停戦監視団を、関係当事者の同意を得て現地に派遣し、停戦や軍の撤退の監視等を行うことで事態の鎮静化や紛争の再発防止にあたるものです。米ソ冷戦の終結にともなう国連の役割の高まりと共に、国連平和維持活動への需要が高まりました。1948年以降に設立されたPKOは計49件(1998年7月現在)になりますが、そのうち実に36件が1988年以降に設立されています。1998年7月現在、17件のPKOに76ヵ国、約1万5000人が参加しています。

1992年6月には「国際平和協力法」が制定され、PKOへの参加が本格化し、現在までに同法に基づき5件の協力を行ってきています。そのうち、1992年〜93年に設立され、

In recent years, the Security Council has been discussing not only questions of how to deal with disputes and cases of aggression, but also problems brought about by such conflicts, including issues of human rights, refugees and the environment.

The Security Council cannot, however, carry out truly legitimate and effective actions without the participation of countries which are both willing and able to play global roles. Reflecting the overall increase in the number of UN members, a need for increasing the number of seats in the Security Council has been pointed out.

Q What roles do UN Peacekeeping Operations play in the world?

United Nations Peacekeeping Operations (PKO) are meant to help calm down tense situations or to prevent recurrence of conflicts by dispatching to the field peacekeeping forces and military observer missions consisting of personnel provided by member states with the consent of the conflicting parties to monitor cease-fires, separation of forces, etc. With the expansion of the role of the United Nations after the end of the Cold War, there grew a stronger need for UN Peacekeeping Operations. Since 1948 when the first PKO was instituted, there have been 49 peacekeeping missions (as of July 1998), of which 36 were set up after 1988. As of July 1998, approximately 15,000 personnel from 76 countries were participating in 17 PKOs.

Since the enactment of the Law Concerning Cooperation for United Nations Peacekeeping Operations and Other Operations ("International Peace Cooperation Law") in June 1992, Japan has participated in five PKOs under this

カンボジアでの議会選挙実施など大規模な活動を行った「国連カンボジア暫定統治機構」(UNTAC)には、停戦監視要員、文民警察要員、施設部隊など、延べ1200名を超える人員が日本から参加しました。

また現在、日本はシリアのゴラン高原に展開中の「国連兵力引き離し監視軍」(UNDOF)に自衛隊から45名の要員を派遣しており、司令部業務や輸送等の後方支援業務に従事しています。

なお、日本の国連PKO活動経費の分担率は15.66%（97年1月現在）であり、通常分担金と同様、米国に次ぐ世界第2位の分担率となっています。

Q 日本は「世界平和」のためにどんな役割が期待されているのでしょうか。また具体的にどの分野で役割を果たしているのでしょうか。

日本は、第2次大戦終了後50年余にわたり、西側陣営にあって未曾有の繁栄を享受してきました。その結果、今や世界のGDPの約18%、世界の対直接投資残高の約16%、世界の輸出額の約9%、輸入額の約7%を占める大国になりました。しかし、資源に乏しく、国土も人口に比して狭小な日本のこのような繁栄は、世界の平和と安定があってこそのことです。

law so far. Over 1,200 personnel from Japan took part as cease-fire monitors, civilian police personnel, engineering units, etc., in the activities of UNTAC (the United Nations Transitional Authority in Cambodia) which was set up during 1992-1993 and oversaw such large-scale activities as the National Assembly elections.

45 members of Japan Self-Defense Forces are currently dispatched to UNDOF (the United Nations Disengagement Observer Force) on the Golan Heights, Syria, and are engaged in secondary support for staff activities and for transportation.

As of January 1997 Japan's assessed contribution to the budget for the United Nations peacekeeping activities was 15.66%. Like its assessed contribution to the UN regular budget, this portion is the second largest, next to that of the United States.

Q What sorts of roles are expected of Japan in the interests of world peace? In what specific areas is Japan performing such roles?

In the course of the more than 50 years since the end of the Second World War, Japan, as a member of the Western camp, came to enjoy prosperity as never before. As a result, it has become a very large country in the sense that its gross domestic product (GDP) is about 18% of the total of all countries' GDPs taken together. Its direct overseas investments are about 16% of the world total, while its exports and imports are approximately 9% and 7%, respectively, of the world totals. The fact that Japan is densely populated while lacking in natural resources is all the more reason why its prosperity depends on world peace and stability.

　また、政治的・経済的な影響力を持つ国となった日本が、国際社会で責任ある役割を果たしていくことは、21世紀における世界の平和と安定に大きな意味を持っており、国際社会が抱える諸問題に日本がより一層取り組んでいくことが、我が国自身のためのみならず世界全体からも期待されております。

　世界平和・安定のための日本の協力としては、まず、国連安保理で、最多の8回目の非常任理事国を務め、国連平和維持活動(PKO)に積極的に参加し、世界第2位の国連分担金(我が国の通常分担率は97年17.981%、98年19.981%、2000年20.573%)を負担しています。

Ogata Sadako (UN High Commissioner for Refugees)

　また日本は、カンボジア和平、旧ユーゴスラビア和平、中東和平にも、ヒト、モノ、カネの面で支援を行ったほか、北朝鮮の核エネルギー開発問題や食糧援助問題、ロシアの改革などについても、国際機関、G8や韓国等と協力してきています。さらに途上国の経済発展が世界平和にとっての基礎になるとの観点から、政府開発援助を行っているほか、世界各国の相互文化理解および人類の文化遺産の未来への継承の観点から国際文化交流にも取り組んでいます。

Akashi Yasushi (former UN Vice Secretary-General)

　そして、日本からは緒方貞子国連難民高等弁務官、明石康国連事務次長(当時)、小

Japan is today a country with much political and economic influence, and its playing a responsible role in international society is of great significance for world peace and stability in the 21st century. Japan's further involvement in dealing with various problems confronting the international community is expected by the whole world, and it is also in the interests of Japan.

As an example of Japan's cooperation in the pursuit of world peace and stability, there is first of all its often-exercised role as one of the nonpermanent members of the United Nations Security Council. It served in this position for the eighth time during the period 1996–98, the greatest number of times any nonpermanent member has served. We must also mention Japan's active participation in United Nations Peacekeeping Operations and the fact that Japan provides the second largest share of United Nations expenses (Japan's share of assessments within the regular operating budget was 17.981% in 1997, 19.981% in 1998, and is expected to be 20.573% in 2000).

In addition to assisting with money, materials, and personnel in UN-sponsored peace processes in Cambodia, the former Yugoslavia and the Middle East, Japan has cooperated with other international organizations, the G-8 countries, and South Korea in supporting reforms in Russia and in providing food aid to North Korea and helping finance its development of nuclear energy for peaceful purposes. Because of its views that the economic development of the developing countries is fundamental to world peace, Japan carries out programs of Official Development Assistance (ODA). Japan is also engaged in programs of international cultural exchange aiming to encourage cultural understanding among the world's countries and to help transmit mankind's cultural legacies to future generations.

A number of Japanese are actively at work in important posts in international organizations. Among them are United

田滋国際司法裁判所裁判官、山本草二国際
海洋法裁判所裁判官などの人々が国際機関
に入って活躍しているほか、非政府団体
(NGO)のメンバーやボランティアとして
様々な日本人が国際的な舞台で活躍してい
ます。

Q 難民の救済のために、日本はどのように 取り組んでいるのですか。

東西冷戦構造に封じ込められていた各地
域の民族対立、宗教的対立等が、冷戦終結
後のタガの外れにより表面化し、紛争が続発
してきました。そして、その紛争がもたらす
戦火や迫害から避難する難民の数が激増し
ました。

1980年に約1000万人だった難民数は、
1995年には、その3倍の約3000万人に達
しましたが、その後インドシナ難民の減少、
モザンビークおよびルワンダ難民の帰還によ
り、1997年には2300万人となっています。
地域別ではアフリカが最大でアジアとヨーロ
ッパがそれに続いています。
しかし、難民問題は特定の国家間の援助
によって解決される問題ではありません。そ
のために、国連難民高等弁務官事務所
(UNHCR)、世界食糧計画(WFP)、赤十字
国際委員会(ICRC)、国連パレスチナ難民救
済事業機関(UNRWA)等の国際機関やNGO
が、難民支援に大きな役割を果たしていま
す。

Nations High Commissioner for Refugees Ogata Sadako, former United Nations Vice Secretary-General Akashi Yasushi, Judge Oda Shigeru at the International Court of Justice, and Judge Yamamoto Sōji at the International Tribunal for the Law of the Sea. In addition, a large number of Japanese are active on the international stage as members and volunteers in a variety of nongovernmental organizations (NGOs).

Q In what ways does Japan assist refugees?

In various regions of the world, confrontations based on ethnic or religious differences that had been held in check by the Cold War structure have tended, in the less-restrained post-Cold War circumstances, to come to the surface, and have even resulted in conflicts. The number of refugees fleeing from the fighting and persecution caused by such conflicts has greatly increased.

The number of refugees reached 30 million in 1995, tripling from 10 million in 1980. However, with the reduction of Indochina refugees and the repatriation of refugees from Mozambique and Rwanda, the figure was brought down to around 23 million as of 1997. The region of the world with the greatest number is Africa, followed by Asia and Europe.

Refugee issues cannot be solved by assistance from only a limited number of countries. Therefore, key roles in assisting refugees are being carried out by the Office of the United Nations High Commissioner for Refugees (UNHCR), the World Food Program (WFP), the International Committee of the Red Cross (ICRC), the United Nations Relief and Works Agency for Palestine Refugees in the Near East (UNRWA), and other international organiza-

日本はこれらの国際機関へ積極的に資金協力を行っているほか、海外で難民支援活動をしている日本のNGOに、NGO事業補助金、草の根無償資金協力、国際ボランティア貯金などを通じて支援をしています。日本政府は1995年11月に、UNHCRと共同でクロアチアに難民のためのシェルターを開設しましたが、その維持・運営には日本のNGOが中心となってあたりました。

さらに、国際平和協力法に基づき、人道的な国際救援活動として、1994年9月には、ルワンダに自衛隊員等約400名を派遣しました。また、日本はインドシナ難民約1万人

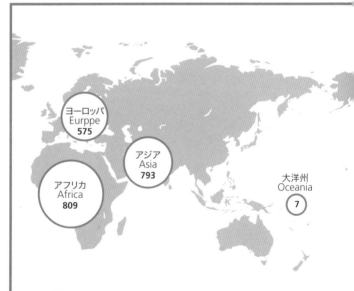

ヨーロッパ
Eurppe
575

アジア
Asia
793

アフリカ
Africa
809

大洋州
Oceania
7

世界の難民情勢 単位:万人
Numbers of Refugees Unit: ten thousands of people

tions and NGOs.

The Japanese government, besides playing an active role in the financing of intergovernmental organizations, also supports Japan-based NGOs that are engaged in assisting refugees overseas through various forms of aid such as NGO activity subsidies, grassroots grant aid, and the International Volunteer Postal Savings Program. In November 1995, the Japanese government established, in cooperation with the UNHCR, shelters for refugees in Croatia, and Japanese NGOs subsequently played a key role in their maintenance and management.

In keeping with the provisions of the International Peace Cooperation Law, 400 Self-Defense Forces personnel were sent to Rwanda in September 1994 to engage in humanitarian international relief operations. The Japanese

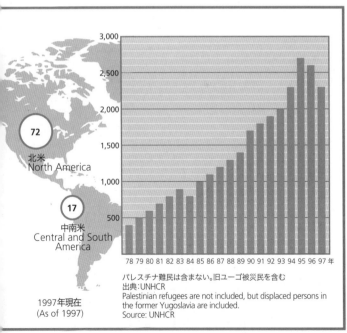

72
北米
North America

17
中南米
Central and South America

1997年現在
(As of 1997)

3,000
2,500
2,000
1,500
1,000
500

78 79 80 81 82 83 84 85 86 87 88 89 90 91 92 93 94 95 96 97 年

パレスチナ難民は含まない。旧ユーゴ被災民を含む
出典:UNHCR
Palestinian refugees are not included, but displaced persons in the former Yugoslavia are included.
Source: UNHCR

の定住を受け入れてきています。

Q 難民分野での日本のNGOの活動は、具体的にどんなものですか。

　国際社会においては、従来は、国や国際機関に属する人たちが活動していましたが、現在では、それらの人たちに加えて、NGOが活動の完全な一員となっています。日本のNGOも海外で活躍してきており、特に国家間あるいは国家内での政治的対立・紛争から発生する難民問題の緩和では、NGOの活動が非常に活発です。

　たとえば、旧ユーゴ、ソマリア、ルワンダ、タンザニアなどで活躍した難民を助ける会、そしてアジアの医師を中心に1984年に設立され、アジア・アフリカ・南米・欧州で医療救援活動を行うアジア医師連絡協議会(AMDA)があります。さらに、立正佼成会、国境なき奉仕団、日本国際救援行動委員会、JHP・学校をつくる会など5つの国内NGO団体で構成され、特に旧ユーゴで活動する日本NGO緊急援助チーム(JEN)があります。

　日本のNGOはまだまだ予算規模も小さく、また日本社会でいまだに顕著な終身雇用制ゆえの人材募集上の問題等もあり、欧米のNGOに比べまだまだ小さいものがほとんどですが、NGOに対する社会の認識も高まってきていますので、難民分野でもより多く

government has granted resettlement in Japan to about 10,000 refugees from Indochina.

Q What are some of the specific features of the refugee-assistance activities of Japanese NGOs?

In addition to persons affiliated with national govern-ments and intergovernmental organizations, today NGOs have become full partners in many activities of the interna-tional community. Some NGOs based in Japan are engaged in activities abroad, their presence being especially prominent in helping alleviate refugee problems caused by political confrontations and conflicts between or within countries.

For example, there is the Association to Aid Refugees, which has been active in the former Yugoslavia, Somalia, Rwanda, and Tanzania, and an emergency assistance group known as Japan Emergency NGOs (JEN), particularly active in former Yugoslavia, composed of the following five Japan-based NGOs: (1) the Association of Medical Doctors of Asia (AMDA), which was founded by Asian doctors in 1984 and engages in medical relief activities in Asia, Africa, South America, and Europe; (2) the Risshō Kōseikai; (3) the Borderless Relief Association in Japan (BRAJA); (4) the Japan International Rescue Action Committee (JIRAC); and (5) the Japan Team of Young Human Power (JHP).

Compared with European and American NGOs, Japan-based NGOs are, for the most part, of relatively small scale with small budgets and, because of the lifetime-employ-ment system still dominant in Japanese society, they often encounter problems in recruiting personnel. However, the recognition given to these NGOs by Japanese society is grow-

の活躍が期待されます。

Q カンボジアやアフガニスタンで
地雷の被害にあう人が後を絶ちませんが、
日本は、その防護、救助のために
何を行っていますか。

　　　　対人地雷は、アンゴラ、アフガニスタン、
カンボジア等の冷戦終焉後の地域紛争等を
中心として、安価に製造できる兵器として紛
争当事者によって無差別に使用、埋設され、
その数は世界で計約1億1000万個以上にの
ぼると言われます。また、対象を選ばずに爆
発し接触した者を殺傷するという性格から一
般市民に対しても無差別に被害を与え、現
在もなお、毎月2000人が死傷していると言
われ、人道上極めて重大な問題となっている
のみならず、紛争終結後の復興と開発にとっ
て大きな障害となっています。
　　この対人地雷問題に対し、我が国も、対人
地雷の禁止のみならず、地雷除去や犠牲者支
援等の国際協力においても、イニシアティブ
を発揮しつつ積極的に取り組んでいます。

　　まず、対人地雷の禁止については、96年6
月リヨン・サミットにおいて、橋本総理（当
時）より、対人地雷に向けた国際的努力を支
持すると共に、我が国としても地雷の使用等
について自主的措置をとることを決定したこ
とを発表しました。その後の軍縮会議および
オタワ・プロセスにおける全面禁止の実現に

ing, and it is expected that they will become even more active
in assisting refugees.

Q People in countries such as Cambodia
and Afghanistan are still being victimized
by landmines. What is Japan doing to
protect and assist these potential and
present landmine victims?

As weapons that can be cheaply manufactured, anti-
personnel landmines have been placed indiscriminately and
left underground mainly in localized conflicts that have continued since the end of Cold War, such as those in Angola,
Afghanistan, Cambodia, and other countries. It is estimated
that the number of landmines remaining in the ground is
more than 110 million around the world today, causing 2,000
civilian casualties a month because of their indiscriminate
nature exploding to kill or wound anyone who happens to
touch them. Not only are landmines a grave concern from
the humanitarian point of view, but they also pose serious
barriers to post-conflict reconstruction.

Japan has been taking positive action on this anti-personnel landmine issue, taking initiatives not only in efforts
to prohibit anti-personnel landmines, but also in international cooperation for demining operations and assistance for
victims.

The then Prime Minister Hashimoto Ryūtarō
announced at the June 1996 Lyon Summit that Japan would
support international efforts toward the banning of anti-personnel landmines, and had decided to take independent measures concerning landmines. Japan actively participated in
international measures toward their total ban in the
Disarmament Conference and the Ottawa Process. Finally,

向けた国際社会の取り組みにも積極的に参加し、最終的に、97年12月の対人地雷禁止条約署名式において同条約に署名しました。

他方、対人地雷の除去および犠牲者支援については、96年6月のリヨン・サミットにおける橋本総理(当時)のイニシアティブを受け、97年3月我が国において「対人地雷に関する東京会議」を開催しました。この東京会議においては、地雷の犠牲者をゼロにすることを国際社会の究極的な目標と定め、今後の国際社会の取り組みを「東京ガイドライン」としてとりまとめました。

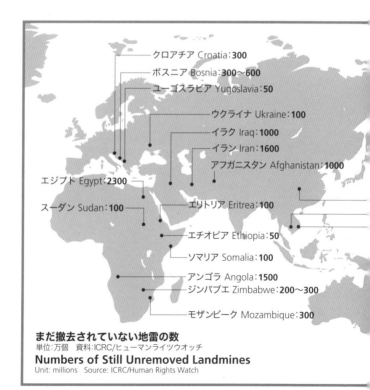

クロアチア Croatia：**300**
ボスニア Bosnia：**300～600**
ユーゴスラビア Yugoslavia：**50**
ウクライナ Ukraine：**100**
イラク Iraq：**1000**
イラン Iran：**1600**
アフガニスタン Afghanistan：**1000**
エジプト Egypt：**2300**
スーダン Sudan：**100**
エリトリア Eritrea：**100**
エチオピア Ethiopia：**50**
ソマリア Somalia：**100**
アンゴラ Angola：**1500**
ジンバブエ Zimbabwe：**200～300**
モザンビーク Mozambique：**300**

まだ撤去されていない地雷の数
単位：万個　資料：ICRC/ヒューマンライツウォッチ
Numbers of Still Unremoved Landmines
Unit: millions　Source: ICRC/Human Rights Watch

Japan signed the Anti-Personnel Landmines Ban Treaty in December 1997.

As regards demining and victim assistance, based on the initiative put forth by Prime Minister Hashimoto at the 1996 Lyon Summit, Japan hosted the Tokyo Conference on Anti-Personnel Landmines in March 1997. In the Tokyo Conference, members drafted the Tokyo Guidelines, establishing "zero victims" as the ultimate goal of international efforts in regard to the anti-personnel landmine issue.

中国 China：**1000**
カンボジア Cambodia：**400〜600**
ベトナム Vietnam：**350**

50万個以上が埋設されたままと思われる地域をあげたが、この他、数は少ないながら、中米、南米北西部、中近東、アフリカの国々の多くに地雷が残っている。

This map points out countries with more than 500,000 buried landmines. However, lesser numbers remain buried in many countries of Central America, north-western South America, the Middle East, and Africa.

　この「東京ガイドライン」をさらに推進するために、1997年12月の対人地雷全面禁止条約署名式の際に、小渕外務大臣（当時）より「犠牲者ゼロ・プログラム」を提唱、2国間援助を含め地雷除去および犠牲者支援の分野での支援を大幅に拡大することとし、今後5年間をめどに100億円程度の支援をODAで行うことを決定、発表しました。その一環として、1998年10月にカンボジア地雷対策センター（CMAC）の主催で開催された、地雷被埋設国間の経験を共有することを目的とするプノンペン・フォーラムを我が国として積極的に支援することを決定しました。

　具体的な支援としては、地雷除去活動については、国連地雷除去信託基金、アフガニスタン難民機関支援基金、カンボジア地雷対策センター等を通じた資金協力としてこれまで10年間で累計約3059万ドルを拠出していますが、今後は、資金拠出に加え、地雷除去関連機材の供与や地雷除去機関の組織強化のための技術協力等も実施していく考えです。また、犠牲者支援としては、草の根無償資金協力やNGOに対する補助金を通じてカンボジアにおける義手義足の製作や犠牲者のリハビリ支援等にこれまで6年間で累計1億55万円（約94万ドル）を拠出していますが、今後はこのような草の根の取り組みを積極的に支援していくとともに、より規模の大きい政府間の支援も行っていく予定です。

To put the Tokyo Guidelines into practice, the then Foreign Minister Obuchi introduced "the Zero Victim Program" during the signing ceremony in Ottawa in December 1997, and announced that Japan would provide a total of around 10 billion yen in assistance through its ODA programs over a five-year period, beginning in 1998, to greatly expand its support, including bilateral assistance, in the fields of mine clearnance and of helping landmine victims. In this connection, Japan decided to actively support the Phnom Penh Forum held under the sponsorship of CMAC in October 1998, for mine-affected countries to share their experience.

As far as concrete assistance for demining activities is concerned, Japan has extended a total of approximately $30.59 million over the past ten years in financial cooperation through the UN Voluntary Trust Fund for Assistance in Mine Clearance, UNOCHA, CMAC, and other agencies. In addition to these financial contributions, in the future Japan intends to provide devices and necessary equipment for mine-clearance activities, technical cooperation for the organizational strengthening of demining agencies, and so on. As for assistance to victims, Japan has provided a total of ¥100.55 million (approximately US $940,000) over the past six years in assistance for such things as the production of artificial hands and limbs and rehabilitation of mine victims in Cambodia through Japan's Grant Assistance for Grassroots Projects and the Subsidy System for NGO Projects. In the future, Japan intends to actively support these kinds of grassroots efforts, as well as extend intergovernmental assistance on an even greater scale.

Q アジア太平洋地域の
平和と安定のために、
日本はどのような貢献をしているのですか。

アジア太平洋──この地域は、現在、経済
的に急成長し、21世紀には世界経済そして
政治の中心となると目されています。しか
し、これが実現するには、大前提として、こ
の地域が平和と安定を維持していくことが必
要です。

冷戦後の今日も、この地域は依然不確
実・不安定要素を抱えています。日本の安定
だけでなくアジア太平洋地域の平和と安定
には、抑止力を持ち、それでいて領土的野望
を持たず、社会も透明度が高いと政治的信
頼を得ている米国が深く関与していることが
不可欠です。日米安全保障条約を基礎とし
た日本と米国の強い協力関係が維持され、
米軍のこの地域におけるプレゼンスが確保さ
れていることが、アジア太平洋地域の平和と
繁栄にも貢献しているのです。

また、日米、米韓、米豪など、米国を中
心に張り巡らされた2国間の安全保障条約を
補完するものとして、中国、ロシアを含むア
ジア太平洋諸国が一堂に会するASEAN地域
フォーラム(ARF)が開かれており、各国が国
防政策を開示し、対話を強化し、人的な交
流を増大するなど、お互いの信頼をかもしだ
す措置が推進されてきています。日本もこの
ARFの有力なメンバーの一員として、この
ような地域協力の枠組みの発展に中心的な
役割を果たしています。

Q What kinds of contributions is Japan making to peace and stability in the Asia-Pacific Region?

The Asia-Pacific region is at present growing very fast economically and is seen by some as the center of the world economy and politics in the 21st century. However, for this to become a reality, the region must continue to maintain peace and stability.

Even today, despite the end of the Cold War, there remain in this region elements of uncertainty and instability. Indispensable to the stability of Japan and to the peace and stability of the Asia-Pacific region is continued deep involvement by the United States, a country with military deterrent capability but without any territorial ambitions that has attained other countries' political trust and has a relatively transparent society. Maintenance of a firm cooperative relationship between Japan and the United States is being maintained, with the Treaty of Mutual Cooperation and Security between Japan and the United States of America at its base, and the ensured presence of US military forces in this region has contributed to the peace and prosperity of the Asia-Pacific region.

To supplement the bilateral security treaties between the United States and other Asia-Pacific countries including Japan, South Korea and Australia, the ASEAN Regional Forum (ARF), where many Asia-Pacific nations including China and Russia meet, has been held to promote confidence-building measures such as the explanation of each member country's national defense policy, the strengthening of dialogues among the members, and the increase of personnel exchanges among them. As an important member of the ARF, Japan is playing a key role in developing this sort of regional cooperation framework.

　また経済の面でも、1989年に発足したア
ジア太平洋経済協力(APEC)フォーラムが、
1994年のインドネシアのボゴール会議にお
いて、先進メンバーは2010年、途上メンバ
ーは2020年までの、自由で開かれた貿易と
投資を達成するという目標を示し、その実現
に向けて、1995年の大阪行動指針、1996
年のマニラ行動計画を通じ、実際に動き出
しています。

　さらに1996年に、アジアとヨーロッパの
25ヵ国の首脳に加えて欧州委員会議長の出
席のもとにバンコクで第1回会合が開催され
たアジア欧州会議(ASEM)も、ヨーロッパと
アジアの21世紀に向けての協力関係を創り
出していこうとしていますが、日本はアジ
ア・太平洋コミュニティの有力な一員とし
て、ARF、APECやASEMのような協力の
場を盛り立てています。

On the economic scene, the Asia-Pacific Economic Cooperation (APEC) forum, which was established in 1989, has put forth as a policy goal (announced at its meeting in Bogor, Indonesia, in 1994) the achievement of free and open trade and investment by 2010 in the case of the developed economies and by 2020 in the case of the developing countries. The APEC participants have been moving in concrete ways toward the realization of this goal in accordance with the Osaka Action Agenda approved in 1995 and the Manila Action Plan for APEC adopted in 1996.

In addition, the inaugural Asia-Europe Meeting (ASEM), which was held in Bangkok in 1996 and was attended by the heads of state and government from 25 nations in Asia and Europe plus the President of the European Commission, is designed to build cooperative relationships between Europe and Asia as we enter the 21st century. Japan, as an important member of the Asia-Pacific community, is making various efforts to ensure the success of ARF, APEC, ASEM, and other forums of cooperation.

人物紹介	カンボジアで 国連ボランティアとして 働く

カンボジアで国連ボランティアとして働く

長く続いたカンボジアの内戦にようやく終止符が打たれ、1992年の1月、国連カンボジア暫定統治機構（UNTAC）の監視下で、カンボジアは統一国家建設の作業に入りました。そして、1993年5月に選挙が行われることになり、その選挙を無事に終わらせるために、世界中から多くのボランティアが派遣されてきました。その中の1人として阪口さんの姿がありました。

阪口さんの小さな時からの夢は、海外に出ていくことで、大学4年生の時、就職活動を捨て、ヨーロッパ、モロッコ、インド、ネパール、東南アジアの国々を回るという大旅行をしました。

1988年には大学を出て、カメラ・光学機器の会社に就職し、海外輸出部に配属され、中国担当となりました。そして、中国に出張したりするのですが、仕事のために海外へ行くだけでは物足りず、連休や休暇を利用しては、仕事を離れいろいろな開発途上国を旅して回っていました。

そして、1992年4月、ふと新聞で目にしたのが、国連ボランティア計画の選挙監視要員募集の広告でした。阪口さんは即座に応募を決心しました。

書類選考、面接を経て、阪口さんは五十数人を超す応募者の中から選ばれました。選ばれたのは29人でした。その中に中田厚仁（なかた・あつひと）さんがいました。中田さん

国連ボランティア
さかぐち なおと
阪口直人
Sakaguchi Naoto
UN Volunteer

Working in Cambodia as a UN Volunteer

After the drawn-out Cambodian civil war finally came to an end, in January 1992 Cambodia began building a unified country under the supervision of the United Nations Transitional Authority in Cambodia (UNTAC). It was decided that elections would be held in May 1993, and volunteers were sent from all over the world to ensure that these elections would be free and fair. Among these volunteers was Mr. Sakaguchi.

Ever since he was a small child, one of Mr. Sakaguchi's dreams was to travel overseas, and when he was a 4th year university student he decided to postpone looking for a permanent job and to go, instead, on a long trip that took him to Europe, Morocco, India, Nepal, and countries of Southeast Asia.

When he graduated from the university in 1988, he joined the export division of a company specializing in cameras and optical equipment, in charge of exports to China. He made several business trips to China, but came to feel unsatisfied with going abroad merely for work. So he began using holidays and other periods of vacation to travel, apart from work assignments, in many developing countries.

In April 1992, Mr. Sakaguchi noticed in a newspaper an advertisement recruiting electoral supervisors for a UN volunteer project. He immediately decided to apply.

After submitting written materials and appearing for an interview, Mr. Sakaguchi was selected as one of 29 successful applicants from among more than 50 who applied. Among the other successful applicants was Nakata Atsuhito,

人物
紹介

は後に、任務中、不幸にも銃で撃たれて亡くなっています。彼は日本が海外に派遣したボランティアの、初の犠牲者でした。

クメール語の特訓など2ヵ月間の研修期間を経て、阪口さんはカナダ人の仲間と、ラタナキリ(Rattanak Kiri)という、北東の国境の地域に派遣されることになりました。そこは少数民族が住む地域で、クメール語も通じないという辺境です。

辺地での仕事は想像を絶する困難さでした。なにしろ選挙なんて初めてのことだし、なんのために選挙するのか理解してもらうだけでも厄介です。それに、密林の奥深くに住む住民たちを探し出し、1人1人の名前、年齢などを聞いて、選挙のために登録しなければなりません。ベトナムやラオスの国境近くに住んでいて、生まれた場所さえはっきりしない人たちも多かったのです。

1993年5月28日、選挙は無事終了し、6月の末、任務を終えた阪口さんは日本に帰ってきましたが、1994年の4月から、今度はモザンビークの選挙監視ボランティアとして派遣されました。そして今、阪口さんは外国語専門学校で、英語を教えたり、開発途上国が抱えている様々な問題について講義をしたりするかたわら、NGOを組織して、カンボジアやミャンマーの視力障害者、地雷の被害者のための学校づくりの支援などをしています。

Mr. Sakaguchi explaining about elections to local residents

who unfortunately would later die from a gunshot wound during his tour of duty. He was the first victim among the volunteers Japan sent overseas.

After two months of special training in the Khmer language, Mr. Sakaguchi was sent, together with colleagues from Canada, to an area called Rattanak Kiri near Cambodia's northeastern border. This is a remote region, inhabited by a minority ethnic group most of whom do not understand Khmer.

His work in this remote area was much more difficult than he had imagined. It was, after all, the first time an election had ever been held there, and it was not easy, first of all, to get people to understand what elections were for. Then he had to go deep into the jungle to search for residents and register them for the election by asking each person's name and age. A lot of the people living near the borders with Vietnam and Laos were not even sure where they were born.

The elections in Cambodia were successfully carried out on May 28, 1993, and at the end of June, Mr. Sakaguchi, having completed his duty, returned to Japan. Later, in April 1994, he was again sent as a volunteer to monitor elections, this time in Mozambique. Today, Mr. Sakaguchi teaches English at a school specializing in foreign languages and gives lectures on the various sorts of problems that are being faced by developing countries. Besides this, he has organized an NGO that builds schools and gives other types of help for people in Cambodia and Myanmar who are visually impaired or who have been victims of land mines.

世界経済の発展の
ために
For the Development
of the World's
Economy

Chapter

Q 今、世界経済に
どんな問題がありますか。

現在の世界経済はグローバル化、ボーダレ
ス化という大きな潮流の中にあります。これ
は冷戦の終結により、旧東側諸国が一斉に
自由主義経済システムの導入を積極的に進
めるとともに、中国、東南アジア諸国が急速
に近代化を遂げ、自由市場経済に参入して
きていることに加え、情報通信技術の飛躍的
発展に拠るものです。こうした動きは、世界
規模での貿易と投資の増大を生み、各国の
相互依存関係を深めます。

Birmingham Summit, 1998 ▲
©Reuters•Sun•Mainichi

Q What sorts of problems exist in the global economy?

Today's world economy is in the midst of powerful currents leading in the direction of globalization and a borderless system of economic transactions. This has been made possible by the fact that the former East-bloc countries, with the conclusion of the Cold War, are all eagerly promoting the introduction of a free market economy, by the fact that China and the countries of Southeast Asia are rapidly modernizing and participating in free market economies, and by the extraordinary development of informational and communications technology. These trends have given rise to an increase in trade and investments on a global scale and are deepening interdependent relationships among countries.

　しかし、利害関係が一層複雑化すると同時に経済競争を激化させる可能性があります。現在、欧州、北米、アジア・太平洋地域に見られる地域経済圏形成の動きは域内の規模の経済・産業の競争力強化や構造調整の進展などを通じて、域内圏の経済を活性化させるものであり、その効果が波及することにより、世界経済全体の発展に寄与することが期待されています。

　しかしながら、こうした地域経済圏が保護主義的な色彩を帯びる可能性も否めません。自由貿易体制の維持・発展は健全な世界経済の前提条件であり、開発途上国や旧東側諸国を国際経済システムに組み入れていくとともに、開かれた地域協力を推進しながら自由で多角的な貿易体制をどのように作り上げて国際社会の安定と繁栄を実現させるかが世界経済における最大の課題と言えましょう。

　しかし、戦後、自由貿易体制を一貫して支えてきた米国経済は、かつての勢いを失い、十分なリーダーシップを発揮することは出来ず、むしろ保護主義的な貿易政策すら採る傾向にあります。また、米国経済の衰退とともに、それまで基軸通貨であったドルに対する信頼性も薄れつつあります。高度成長経済下にあった東南アジア各国においても、自国通貨の下落による通貨不安といった現象も生まれています。健全な貿易と投資を促進するためには通貨と金融市場の安定を維持していくための国際的なシステムの整備を図ることがこれまで以上に重要にな

However, as relationships affecting economic interests become more complex, there is the possibility that this process could cause increased frictions in international competition for markets. The trends seen toward the integration of regional economies, in Europe, North America, and the Asia-Pacific region bring added vigor to these regions' economies by increasing, on an intraregional scale, economic and industrial competition, and by encouraging intraregional structural adjustments. It is to be expected that, as the effects of these trends spread, they will contribute to the progress of the world economy as a whole.

It cannot be denied, however, that regional economies could possibly assume a protectionist coloration. The maintenance and development of a free trading system is a precondition for a sound world economy, and the question of how to incorporate the developing countries and the former East-bloc countries into the international economic system, as well as the question of how to bring stability and prosperity to international society by building a multilateral free trading system (while at the same time promoting open regional cooperation), may be called the most important tasks for the world economy.

The United States' economy, which has continuously supported the free trading system over the decades since the Second World War, is losing some of its former vigor and cannot exert its leadership to the extent that it once did. It is in fact showing tendencies to adopt trade policies that are rather protectionist. With the relative decline of the United States' economy, confidence in the dollar, which has heretofore been the world's standard currency, is weakening. Even in Southeast Asian countries that have enjoyed rapid economic growth, we see the phenomenon of currency instability and declines in the values of these countries' currencies. In order to promote sound trade and investment, it has become more important than ever before to create

っています。

　東アジア諸国をはじめとして一部の開発
途上国が順調な成長を遂げる中で、南北問
題、南南問題といった成長格差の問題も依
然として存在しています。先進諸国は成長
格差の問題に対処するためこれまで資金協
力や技術協力を行ってきましたが、国・地
域によっては必ずしも期待通りの効果が得
られているとは言えず、また、最近では低成
長と失業問題に悩む先進国は援助より自国
経済の建て直しに追われているという厳しい
現状があり、援助資金のより一層効率的・
効果的な活用が重要な課題となっています。
しかも旧東側諸国がスムーズに自由市場経
済に移行するためには先進諸国の援助・協
力が必要不可欠であり、援助の配分につい
ても緊急に解決しなければならない問題と言
えるでしょう。

Q そうした問題を解決するために
どんな努力がなされていますか。
また、日本はどんなことをしていますか。

　1997年6月に開催されたデンバー・サミ
ットでは、世界経済の諸問題解決のための方
策が、主要議題の1つとして、首脳の間で真
剣に議論されました。その結果、市場のグロ
ーバル化が世界の経済成長の重要な推進力
であり、すべての国に機会をもたらすもので
あることが認識された他、(1)各国が引き続
き経済成長を促進するための諸施策を行う

international systems that will effectively contribute to the stability of currencies and financial markets.

As Southeast Asia and a number of other developing countries make progress in achieving steady growth, there continues to be the problem of gaps in growth rates, as reflected in the terms "North-South problem" and "South-South problem." In order to address the issue of gaps in growth rates, the developed countries have extended financial and technical cooperation, but it cannot be said that the results in all countries and regions have met expectations. In recent years, many developed countries suffering from problems of low growth and unemployment have felt pressured to pay more attention to rebuilding their own economies than to providing aid to others; hence an important task is to find ways of using assistance funds more efficiently and effectively. Moreover, for the former East-bloc countries to make a smooth transition to a free market economies, assistance and cooperation from the developed countries will be indispensable. Another important matter that must be quickly resolved is the geographical distribution of assistance funds.

Q What kinds of efforts are being made to solve these problems?
And what is Japan doing about them?

At the Denver Summit held in June 1997, one of the main things that the participating heads of state discussed with much seriousness was policies for resolving problems in the world economy. While it was recognized that the globalization of markets is an important stimulus to world economic growth providing worthwhile opportunities to all countries, it was also reiterated that: (1) each country should continue to take measures to promote its own economic growth; (2)

こと、(2)グローバルな金融システムの強化のために国際協調を行うこと、(3)統合された世界経済構築のために各国が協力して課題を克服することなどが再確認されました。

デンバー・サミットにおいて、日本は規制制度改革をはじめとする構造改革を推進することを表明するとともに、雇用に関する国際会議の日本での開催を提唱しました。

この他、経済協力開発機構(OECD)、世界貿易機関(WTO)、国際通貨基金(IMF)等の国際機関において、世界経済の安定・成長促進、多角的自由貿易体制の維持・強化、国際金融秩序の維持といった諸問題解決のための方策が検討されています。こうした機関に対して、日本は高い分担金を拠出する他、松下満雄成蹊大学教授がWTO上級委員会委員として紛争解決に従事する等、多くの日本人が活躍しています。

日本は多角的自由貿易体制の最大の受益者の1つです。戦後、日本は産業の高度化を図り、輸出品の付加価値を高め、めざましい発展を遂げました。無論これは日本自身の努力に拠るところも大きいのですが、自由かつ多角的な貿易体制の中で、世界の貿易・経済が拡大し、それを基礎に国際社会の安定が確保されてきたことも大きな理由です。そうしたことから日本は国際経済の世界的な協調と安定的発展に向けて指導力を発揮することが期待されています。

there should be international coordination to strengthen global financial systems; and (3) all countries should cooperate to overcome the problems of building a more unified world economy.

At the Denver Summit, Japan announced that it would promote structural reforms (including changes in its regulatory systems) and proposed the holding in Japan of an international conference on employment.

International bodies such as the Organization for Economic Cooperation and Development (OECD), the World Trade Organization (WTO), and the International Monetary Fund (IMF), are exploring ways to resolve various problems, with a view to promoting stability and growth of the world economy, maintaining and strengthening a multilateral free trading system, and maintaining order in international financial transactions. To support the work of these international bodies, Japan provides a large share of their operating budgets and many Japanese are active as staff personnel, such as Seikei University Professor Matsushita Mitsuo, who is serving on the Appellate Body of the Dispute Settlement Body of the WTO.

Japan is one of the prime beneficiaries of the multilateral free trading system. After World War II, Japan strove to upgrade its industries, improved the value-added segment of its exports, and achieved outstanding economic progress. Of course much of this success can be attributed to Japan's own efforts, but a key factor is that world trade and the world economy expanded under a system of free and multilateral trade, which formed a solid basis for the preservation of stability in international society. Given this historical experience, Japan is expected to exercise leadership in the quest for stable development and international coordination of the global economy.

Q 世界経済の維持・発展のために
国際機関に日本はどのように
関わっていますか。

　　世界経済の発展に貢献している主要な国際機関としてはOECD、WTO、IMF、世界銀行等があげられます。

　　1961年に発足したOECDは、加盟国の協力による経済の安定成長と貿易拡大、さらに加盟国による開発途上国援助の促進と自由な国際経済の交流を主な目的としています。日本は分担金の4分の1弱を負担(加盟国中第2位)する他、重原久美春事務次長など幹部ポストを中心とした人的な貢献を行っています。

　　ウルグアイ・ラウンド(多角的貿易交渉)のマラケシュ会議で創設が決まったWTOは1995年に、新しい世界貿易秩序の構築を目指して発足しました。WTOでは、これまでのGATT(関税と貿易に関する一般協定)と比較して、(1)サービス貿易、知的所有権などの新しい分野も対象とされ、(2)紛争解決メカニズムが大幅に強化・改善されるとともに、(3)GATTでは加盟国ごとにバラバラに締結されていた諸協定が一括して運用されることになる等の特徴を持ちます。日本は米、EU、カナダとともにいわゆる四極の一員としてWTOにおける協議に積極的に貢献するとともに、米、独に次ぐ分担金を負担しています。

　　1945年に国際通貨体制の安定と戦後復興を目的として設立された、IMFと国際復興開発銀行(IBRD、通称「世界銀行」)も戦後一貫して世界経済の発展に貢献してきた国際

Q In what ways does Japan participate in intergovernmental bodies to support and develop the global economy?

Among major intergovernmental bodies contributing to the development of the global economy we must list, first of all, the OECD, the WTO, the IMF, and the World Bank.

The main goals of the OECD, which was inaugurated in 1961, are stable economic growth and expanded trade, through cooperation among its member countries, free international economic exchange, and assistance to developing countries. Japan contributes a little less than one-fourth of the operating budget—the second largest share among the member countries—and provides several staff members, including Deputy Secretary-General Shigehara Kumiharu .

The WTO, whose establishment was decided upon at the Marrakech Meeting of the GATT Uruguay Round, began its work aimed at the building a new world trade order in 1995. Compared to the GATT (General Agreement on Tariffs and Trade) organization that preceded it, the WTO has several distinguishing features, including (1) attention to such new issues as trade in services and intellectual property rights; (2) greatly improved and strengthened dispute settlement mechanisms; and (3) the fact that various agreements are applied collectively to all the Members although they had been applied separately to specific Members under the GATT. Japan, as one of the so-called Quad Members (together with the United States, the European Union, and Canada), plays an active part in WTO deliberations and is the third largest contributor to its operating budget (after the United States and Germany).

The IMF and the IBRD (International Bank for Reconstruction and Development, or "World Bank"), which were established in 1945 to aid postwar reconstruction and the stabilization of the international currency system, have con-

機関です。現在のIBRDは開発途上国の開発のための融資を主たる業務としていますが、累積債務問題に対応するための融資も行うようになっています。

また、IMFでは所得水準の低い開発途上国やロシア等の計画経済から市場経済への移行を進めている諸国に対し援助を行うため、新たな融資制度を創設するなどしています。日本はIBRD、IMFに多額の出資(加盟国中第2位の出資率)を行うとともに、人的貢献も行っています。

Q これら国際機関で日本人はどのような活躍をしていますか。

国際機関への財政的貢献に比して、日本の人的貢献は必ずしも十分なものとは言えませんが、近年では日本人職員の数も徐々に増えつつあります。

OECDでは現在52名(特別職を含む正規職員数・97年9月現在)の邦人職員がおり、うち10名が課長以上の幹部ポストで活躍しています。1995年に発足したWTOでは、日本人職員は4名と少ない状況ですが、98年9月現在、金融サービス交渉に関する委員会などの議長を日本人が務めているほか、紛争処理機関の7名の上級委員会委員のうちの1人として松下満雄成蹊大学教授が活躍しているのが注目されます。

IMFでは約30名の日本人職員が、IBRD

tinued to contribute to the development of the world economy. At present, the main function of the IBRD is to make development loans to developing countries, but it also provides funds to help these countries cope with problems of accumulated debt.

The IMF has created new facilities for extending loans to help countries such as Russia in their transition from planned to market economies and the low-income developing countries. Japan provides substantial funding—the second largest share among the member countries—to both the IBRD and the IMF, and also contributes personnel to their projects.

Q In these intergovernmental bodies, what sorts of activities are Japanese engaged in?

Compared to Japan's financial contributions to these international bodies, it cannot necessarily be said that there are at present enough personnel contributions by individuals of Japanese nationality. However, in recent years the numbers of Japanese staff members in these intergovernmental bodies are gradually increasing.

In the OECD, as of September 1997 there were 52 Japanese staff members, including both regular staff and those on special assignment. Among them, 10 were in posts with the rank of director or above. In the WTO, which commenced its work in 1995, there were still only 4 Japanese staff members in the Secretariat as of September 1998, but Japanese are chairing committees including that on financial services negotiations, and Prof. Matsushita Mitsuo of Seikei University is serving as one of the seven members of the WTO's Appellate Body.

In the International Monetary Fund (IMF), there are

では約100名がそれぞれ活躍しています。

Q 世界各地で経済統合の動きが見られますが、なぜですか。これは世界経済の発展につながるのでしょうか。日本のポジションはどのようなものですか。

現在、欧州、北米、アジア・太平洋地域において見られる代表的な地域経済圏には欧州連合(EU)、北米自由貿易協定(NAFTA)、アジア太平洋経済協力会議(APEC)等があります。具体的な内容については各経済圏によって違いはありますが、基本的な考えは同じで、モノ・サービスについて域内取引の障壁を撤廃し、域内での経済活動の活性化を図ろうとするものです。

こうした動きは、冷戦が終結して新しい国際経済秩序の構築を必要とする各国が、周辺地域で経済的結びつきを強化することが自国の繁栄、ひいては世界経済の繁栄と発展に結びつくという認識を有するに至ったことが影響を与えているといえます。地域経済圏での自由な取引は、規模の経済、産業の競争力強化と構造調整の進展などにより域内各国の経済を活性化させるものであり、域外経済にもその効果が波及すれば世界経済の発展にも貢献するものです。

ただし、こうした地域統合は域外国の貿易に悪影響を及ぼす危険性もあるので、地域統

about 30 active Japanese staff members, and in the IBRD there are about 100.

Q Why do we see, throughout the world,
trends toward economic integration?
Do these help efforts to develop
the world's economy?
What is Japan's position on this issue?

At present, the largest and most publicized regional economic groupings are the European Union (EU), the grouping built around the North American Free Trade Agreement (NAFTA), and the grouping built around the Asia-Pacific Economic Cooperation (APEC) forum. Their specific characteristics differ, but their ultimate goal is the same, namely, to provide added vitality to economic activities within each region by removing barriers to intraregional transactions affecting goods and services.

Reflected in these trends is the fact that various countries, feeling the need to build a new international economic order after the conclusion of the Cold War, have come to realize that strengthening economic ties with neighboring regions contributes to their own prosperity and, by extension, to the progress and prosperity of the global economy. Free transactions within a given regional economic grouping stimulate economies in countries throughout the region through economies of scale, the strengthening of industrial competitiveness, progress with structural adjustments, and the like. As positive results extend outward and affect economies outside the region, they contribute to the development of the world economy at large.

However, such processes of regional integration have the potential for negative impacts on the trade of countries

合などがWTO協定に整合的であり、多角的
自由貿易体制を強化・補完するものである
ことを確保する必要があります。そのために
日本はWTOやAPECの場で、地域統合が
域外国に対する障壁を設けたり、世界経済
のブロック化につながったりすることがない
よう積極的な役割を果たしています。

Q APECは、アジア太平洋地域において
どのような役割を果たしているのですか。
APECにおいて日本は
どのような役割を果たしているのですか。

　APECは、自由貿易体制の維持・強化を
積極的に推進し、閉鎖的な貿易ブロック形
成を廃し「開かれた地域協力」を目指して、
1989年のキャンベラでの第1回閣僚会議か
らスタートしました。当初の参加メンバーは
日、米、加、ニュージーランド、豪、韓国、
ASEAN等12ヵ国でしたが、現在は中国、
台湾、メキシコ等が加わり18の国・地域に
より構成されています。98年の閣僚会議か
らはペルー、ロシア、ベトナムが新たに参加
しました。
　89年以後、毎年閣僚会議が開催されまし
たが、93年よりは新たに非公式首脳会議も
加わり、これらの会議により、首脳間でアジ
ア・太平洋地域における経済の現状と課題に
つき共通認識が形成されるとともに、今後の
域内協力について一定の方向性が示され、今
後の活動に大きな弾みを与えることになりま

outside the region in question. Therefore, it is necessary to make efforts to insure that the specifics of regional integration are consistent with WTO agreements and that they strengthen and supplement the multilateral free trading system. In this spirit, Japan, in cooperation with the WTO and APEC, is playing an active role in ensuring that regional integration does not lead to the building of barriers against countries outside a given region or lead toward a division of the world economy into blocs.

Q What sorts of roles does APEC play in the Asia-Pacific region? What kinds of roles does Japan play in APEC?

APEC, which aims at actively maintaining and strengthening the free trade system and "open regionalism" through a rejection of building exclusive trade blocs, had its start with the first ministerial meeting held in Canberra, Australia, in 1989. There were originally 12 participating countries, including Japan, the United States, Canada, New Zealand, Australia, the Republic of Korea, and the members of ASEAN, but after being joined by China, Taiwan, Mexico, and others, the grouping now comprises 18 countries and regions. In addition, Peru, Russia and Vietnam joined APEC starting with the ministerial meeting in 1998.

Since 1989 there have been yearly ministerial meetings, and in addition, since 1993, there have also been informal meetings of APEC-member heads of state. In these meetings common understandings are built up among the heads of states in regard to current economic situations and problems in the Asia-Pacific region. Also at these meetings, general guidelines for future regional cooperation are outlined,

した。

さらに1994年にインドネシア・ボゴール市における非公式首脳会議で採択された「ボゴール宣言」では、先進メンバーは2010年、途上メンバーは2020年までに自由で開かれた貿易・投資の実現という目標が設定されました。

日本はアジア太平洋地域の経済面での協力の中核としてAPECを重視し、APECにおける協力に積極的に取り組んで来ています。中でも95年に大阪で開催された閣僚会議と非公式首脳会議では議長国として、今後のAPECの具体的な行動の戦略的枠組みとも言うべき「大阪行動指針」を打ち出し、加盟国・地域の合意を得ました。

また、94年のジャカルタ閣僚会議で当時の河野外務大臣が提案した、APECにおける経済・技術協力の一層の推進を目的とした「PFP」(前進のためのパートナーシップ)が大阪会議で採択され、96年度には競争政策、基準適合性、工業所有権の3分野の協力が96年度から開始され、2000年度まで継続して実施される予定です。

96年のフィリピン会議においては、全18メンバーが「大阪行動指針」に従い、「個別行動計画」(IAP)を提出、また、「共同行動計画」(CAP)が策定され、「APECマニラ行動計画96」(MAPA96)として採択されました。これは97年1月より実施に移されており、APECは「構想」の段階からいよいよ本格的に「行動」を開始しました。

providing an important stimulus to ensuing activities.

In the "Bogor Declaration" adopted at the informal meeting of heads of state in Bogor, Indonesia, in 1994, the goal of realizing free and open trade and investment among the advanced-economy members by 2010, and among the developing-country members by 2020, was set forth.

Japan has attached great importance to APEC as the core mechanism for economic cooperation within the Asia-Pacific region and has actively participated in it. Japan had the responsibility of chairing both the ministerial meeting and the heads of state meeting held in Osaka in 1995. These meetings formulated and agreed on the Osaka Action Agenda, which might be called a detailed strategic framework of action for APEC in the future.

Also approved at the Osaka meetings was the Partnership for Progress (PFP) plan, originally proposed by former Minister of Foreign Affairs Kōno at the Jakarta ministerial meeting in 1994, as a means of promoting greater economic and technological cooperation among the APEC countries. As a result of this PFP agreement, programs of cooperation in the three fields of competition policy, standards and comformances, and industrial property rights got under way in fiscal 1996 and are planned to continue through fiscal 2000.

At the APEC meetings held in the Philippines in 1996, all 18 members, in accordance with the Osaka Action Agenda, put forth both an Individual Action Plan (IAP) and a Collective Action Plan (CAP), which were adopted as the Manila Action Plan for APEC, 96 (MAPA96). With its establishment in January 1997, APEC has finally moved, in a full-fledged way, from a stage of concepts to one of action.

Q 21世紀のエネルギー事情はどうなるのですか。原子力の平和利用について、世界ではどのような体制がとられているのですか。

現在、エネルギー源として最も広く利用されている石油は、各国の省エネ努力と新規の油田開発や採鉱・生産技術の進歩の結果、確認・可採埋蔵量が大幅に増加したことなどから、21世紀初頭においても引き続き主要なエネルギー源の1つとして利用されることが予想されています。しかし、エネルギーの安定供給の確保や地球環境保護のためには、石油に代わるエネルギー源の開発を推進し、石油への依存度を低めていくことが必要です。こうした観点から国際エネルギー機関(IEA)では、石油火力発電所の新設を禁止したり(1979年)、省エネや下記の新エネルギー開発への取り組みを進めています。

特に、新エネルギーの研究開発については、(1)太陽熱、光(ソーラー)、(2)風力、潮力等の自然エネルギー、(3)オイル・サンド、石炭液化、ガス化等の合成燃料が積極的に検討されています。しかし、まだどの新エネルギーをとっても現実的なコストで大量安定供給のめどがたっているものがないことから、世界のエネルギー供給の構造を長期的に見通せるまでには至っていません。

石油に代わるものとして重要なエネルギー供給源となっている原子力については、軍事目的への転用防止、災害時の対応、廃棄物処理などが大きな課題となっています。1957年に創設されたIAEA(国際原子力機

Q What will the energy situation be like in the 21st century? What sorts of measures are being taken in the world with respect to peaceful uses of nuclear energy?

Due to worldwide efforts to conserve energy and the large increase in proven and recoverable reserves resulting from the development of new oil fields and innovations in exploitation and production technology, it is expected that petroleum, which is the most widely utilized energy source at present, will continue to be the number one energy source in the early 21st century. However, in order to ensure stable energy supplies and to protect the global environment, it will be necessary to lower the degree of reliance on oil and to promote the development of other energy sources. From this perspective, the International Energy Agency (IEA) in 1979 decided to put a stop to the construction of new petroleum-fueled thermal electric power plants and continues to advocate active efforts to conserve energy and to develop new energy sources.

Examples of new energy sources for which research is actively underway are (1) solar energy; (2) other natural energy sources such as wind and tidal power; and (3) synthetic fuels derived from oil sand or by the liquefaction or gasification of coal. However, since goals for a stable supply, in large quantities and at a reasonable cost, of any of these new forms of energy have still not been met, we still do not yet have an adequate long-range view of the economic structure of future world energy supplies.

As for nuclear power, potentially an important source of energy for replacing oil, there are major problems in regard to preventing misuse for military purposes, responding to possible nuclear disasters, and disposing of nuclear wastes. The International Atomic Energy Agency (IAEA), established in

関)は原子力の平和利用を推進するとともに、その利用が軍事目的に転用されないようにコントロールする事を目的としています。

　IAEAは平和利用分野での情報配布、安全基準の設定、条約作成等の幅広い活動を行うとともに、核物質の軍事目的への転用を防ぐための核査察を実施しています。この他IAEAでは原子力発電所の相次ぐ事故から、原発の最低の安全基準を定める原子力安全国際条約を94年に採択し、同条約は96年に発効しています。

1957, exists for the purpose of promoting peaceful uses of nuclear energy and imposing controls to prevent its being turned to military purposes.

The IAEA is engaged in a wide range of activities, including the distribution of information, the setting of safety standards, and the drafting of treaties. It carries out inspections of nuclear power plants to prevent diversion of nuclear materials to military ends. Against the background of a series of accidents at nuclear power stations, the IAEA in 1994 adopted the Nuclear Safety Treaty, which specifies minimum safety standards for nuclear power stations. It went into effect in 1996.

人物紹介

世界の経済摩擦を調停する

1997年、ウイスキーやブランデーの値段が下がり、逆に、焼酎類の値段が上がって、日本の焼酎ファンの人たちを怒らせるということがありました。これは1995年にアメリカ、カナダ、EUが、ウイスキーに対する日本の税額が焼酎類の6倍であることは高すぎると、世界貿易機関（WTO）に提訴し、提訴した国々の主張を認めたWTOの勧告に日本が従って、酒税率を変えたからでした。

1995年に、関税と貿易に関する一般協定（GATT）を格上げする形で発足したWTOは、紛争処理の機能が大幅に強化されており、上のような問題も含めて様々な貿易紛争の解決に取り組んでいます。

貿易問題はまず、紛争当事者の2国間で協議されますが、結論が出なければ紛争処理小委員会（パネル）での協議にかけられます。しかし、その結論にも不満である場合には、さらに上級委員会に提訴することができるのです。この上級委員会の委員の1人として活躍しているのが松下満雄さんなのです。

松下さんがWTOの上級委員に選ばれたのは1995年の12月のことでした。松下さんは東京大学の名誉教授で、今は成蹊大学の法学部で教壇に立ち、また弁護士としても活躍している忙しい身でした。上級委員を引き受ければ、さらに忙しい生活になってしまいます。しかし、松下さんは迷いませんでした。若いころから研究課題にしてきた

世界貿易機関（WTO）上級委員
まつしたみつお
松下満雄

Matsushita
Mitsuo
**Member of
the Appellate
Body of the
World Trade
Organization
(WTO)**

Conciliating Frictions in the World Economy

In 1997 something happened to upset Japan's devotees of *shōchū*: the price of whiskey and brandy dropped, but there was a rise in the price of *shōchū*. In 1995, the United States, Canada, and the EU had lodged complaints with the WTO pointing out that Japan's tax rate for *shōchū* was only one-sixth the rates for imported whiskey. Finally, Japan obeyed the ruling of the WTO, which recognized as valid the arguments of the complainants, and adjusted its taxes on alcoholic beverages.

The WTO was inaugurated in 1995 as an upgraded successor to the General Agreement on Tariffs and Trade (GATT) organization. Its capacities for dealing with trade disputes have been greatly strengthened over those of GATT, and it is currently engaged in resolving various types of trade disputes like the one described above.

Trade problems are first of all discussed bilaterally between the countries which are parties to a dispute, and if a conclusion is not forthcoming, the problem is submitted for further deliberation to a Dispute Resolution Panel. If there are still objections to the panel's conclusions, the problem may be appealed to the WTO's Appellate Body. Matsushita Mitsuo works today as one of the members of this Appellate Body.

Mr. Matsushita was chosen for the Appellate Body in December 1995. At that time he was already a busy person: a professor emeritus of the University of Tokyo, presently a professor in the Law Department of Seikei University and a practicing lawyer. He knew that if he accepted the position on the Appellate Body he would be even busier. He did not hesitate, however, to accept the offer. He was enthusiastic about being able to engage personally, in real-life situations, with topics he

人物紹介

「経済と法律の接点」「国内法秩序と国際社会の接点」という問題に実際に取り組むことができる、という強い意欲で、松下さんは上級委員を引き受けました。

上級委員の数はわずか7人です。世界を大きく7つの地域に分け、それぞれ地域から各1人という配分になっています。そして、7人のうち3人が1つの提訴の審議を担当します。最終的な決定をする前には、全員が集まって討論します。

松下さんが担当した事件で一番印象に残っているのは、EUが、発癌性があるという理由で、ホルモン投与で育てられたアメリカ・カナダの牛肉の輸入を禁止した問題です。アメリカとカナダはこれを不当だとして、WTOに提訴しました。

WTOは1998年初めに、必ずしも発癌性についての根拠がないので、EUの措置はWTO協定に違反すると決定し、EUに対して協定違反を是正するように勧告しましたが、国民の健康を守るという政府の責任と、貿易の自由を確保するという要請とのジレンマにはさまれ、WTOの発足以来、最も難しい事件でした。

WTOへの提訴の数は、1997年には約100件になりました。

The 7 Members of
the WTO Appellate Body.
Mr. Matsushita is second
from the right.

had chosen to do research on since his youth, namely, the
interface between economics and law and the interface
between international society and individual countries' legal
orders.

The WTO's Appellate Body has only seven members, one
to represent each of seven geographical regions of the world.
In any given appellate case, three of the seven members are
charged with making detailed deliberations, although all seven
members must gather for discussions before any final decision
is made.

Mr. Matsushita says the most memorable case he has so
far dealt with an import prohibition, on the part of the European
Union, of U.S. and Canadian meat from cows raised on a hor-
mone-enhanced diet, due to suspicion that such hormones are
possibly cancer-causing substances. The United States and
Canada appealed to the WTO saying the reason for the EU's
prohibition was unfounded.

At the beginning of 1998, the WTO issued a decision that
since there is insufficient evidence that the hormones can cause
cancer, the EU measure was in violation of the WTO Agreement
and that the EU must bring its measure into conformity with
the requirements of the Agreement. This has been, Mr.
Matsushita says, an exceptionally difficult case for the WTO
to deal with since the organization is placed in a dilemma
between governments' responsibilities for protecting the health
of their citizens and the requirements of facilitating free trade.

About 100 trade disputes were submitted to the WTO
during 1997.

開発問題
解決のために
Solving Development-
ment Problems

Ⅲ

Chapter

Q 開発途上国に対する政府開発援助は
なぜ必要なのですか。

　　開発途上国では今なお、10億人以上の
人々が、厳しい貧困の中での生活を余儀な
くされています。また2000年には、途上国
で暮らす人の数が世界の人口の5分の4に達
すると予測されています。途上国の開発の遅
れは、人口問題や食糧危機、政治・経済の
不安定による難民の流出、環境破壊などの
要因となり、先進国に暮らす私たちの生活に
も深刻な影響を及ぼします。したがって、開
発途上国における問題は、単に人道的見地
から見過ごせないだけでなく、政府開発援
助を通じてその克服に貢献することは私たち

APEC meeting, 1998 ▲

Q Why is "development assistance" needed?

In today's so-called developing countries, over one billion people still have no immediate alternative but to live in conditions of extreme poverty. In the year 2000, an estimated four-fifths of the world's people will live in countries classified as "developing." Delays in these countries' development are an important factor behind population problems, food crises and, especially if there is political and/or economic instability, other problems including the destruction of the natural environment and outflows of refugees. All these problems can have serious impacts, even on the lives of people living in developed countries. Thus, while the problems of the developing countries cannot be overlooked from a humanitarian

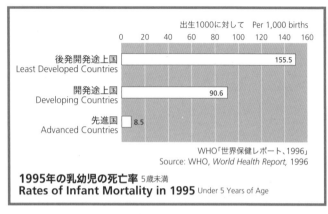

出生1000に対して　Per 1,000 births

| | 0 | 20 | 40 | 60 | 80 | 100 | 120 | 140 | 160 |

後発開発途上国
Least Developed Countries ————— 155.5

開発途上国
Developing Countries ————— 90.6

先進国
Advanced Countries 8.5

WHO「世界保健レポート、1996」
Source: WHO, *World Health Report,* 1996

1995年の乳幼児の死亡率 5歳未満
Rates of Infant Mortality in 1995 Under 5 Years of Age

の生活を守ることにもつながるのです。

　また、開発途上国の経済発展は、最近の東アジアのように、貿易・投資等を通じた経済交流の活発化により、日本を含めた先進国にも大きな利益をもたらしています。さらに、資源小国である日本は、国民生活に必要なエネルギーや食糧等の基礎的な生活物資を、主として開発途上国からの輸入に頼っており、日本にとって、政府開発援助を通じて開発途上国との良好な関係を維持することは、広い意味で日本の安全保障を確保するためにも重要なのです。

Q 日本の援助の代表的な例は
どんなものがありますか。

　日本の政府開発援助(ODA)には、開発途上国に対して直接援助を行う2国間援助と、国際機関を通じた援助があります。2国間援

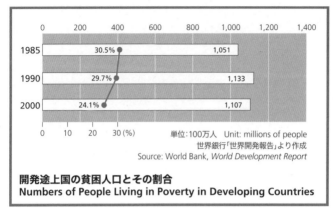

単位：100万人　Unit: millions of people
世界銀行「世界開発報告」より作成
Source: World Bank, *World Development Report*

開発途上国の貧困人口とその割合
Numbers of People Living in Poverty in Developing Countries

point of view, contributions to overcoming these problems through "development assistance" help, at the same time, to protect and sustain our own lives.

Economic progress in the developing countries—as seen, for example, in the East Asian region in recent years — has brought great benefits to developed countries, including Japan, as a result of new stimuli to economic exchange in the forms of trade, investment, etc. Japan is a small country in terms of natural resources and depends to a large extent on developing countries for food and energy resources needed for the daily needs of its people. Japan's use of development assistance as one way of contributing to good relations with developing countries is at the same time important as a means of ensuring Japan's sense of security in the broad sense of the term.

Q What are some important examples of assistance from Japan?

Japan's Official Development Assistance (ODA) comprises both "bilateral assistance," given directly to a developing country, and assistance given through the intermediary

助には「無償資金協力」、「技術協力」、「有
償資金協力」があります。

　無償資金協力は、返済義務を課さずに資
金を供与する援助で、LDC(後発開発途上
国)や財政事情の厳しい途上国を主な対象
とし、医療・保健、衛生、水供給など基礎
生活分野や、教育・研究協力などの人づく
り分野での協力が主要な柱となっています。

　中国の首都北京に日本の無償資金協力で
建設された中日友好病院は、北京有数の設
備を誇る病院として同国の医療の向上に貢
献しています。また、ポリオ根絶を目指しイ
ンドネシア、バングラデシュ等で無償資金協
力により、生ワクチン製造所の建設やワクチ
ンの供与、関連の技術協力が行われていま
す。その他、途上国の債務救済や経済構造
の改善の努力を支援するための資金供与や、
水産業や文化事業の振興のための資金供与
も行っています。

　技術協力は、開発途上国の国づくりを推
進するために、「人づくり」(人材育成と技術
向上)を目的とした援助で、開発途上国から
の研修員の受け入れ❖1や開発途上国への専
門家の派遣❖2、技術移転に必要な機材の供
与がその主な事業となっています。

　また、これら3つを総合的かつ効果的に組
み合わせた協力として、「プロジェクト方式
技術協力」があります。たとえば、ケニアの

of intergovernmental organizations. Bilateral assistance may be in the form of "grant aid," "technical cooperation," or "loan aid."

Grant aid cooperation is assistance in the form of providing grants without repayment. These grants are given mainly to the so-called "Least Developed Countries" (LDCs) and to other developing countries with severe fiscal situations. Important fields for this cooperation are basic human needs such as medical and health services, hygiene, and water supplies, as well as "human resources development," including education and research.

The China-Japan Friendship Hospital in Beijing was constructed with grant aid from Japan. This hospital has some of the best facilities in Beijing, and is contributing much to the improvement of China's medical practices. The procurement of polio vaccine and the construction of local facilities to manufacture live-virus polio vaccines in places like Indonesia and Bangladesh are funded, together with related technical assistance, by Japanese grant aid aimed at eradicating polio. Grant assistance is given to support developing countries' efforts to reform their economic structures and to relieve heavy debts, as well as to promote fisheries and cultural activities.

Technical cooperation is assistance focused on "human resources development" (training of people with specialized skills and knowledge and the raising of technological levels) which promotes the overall development of the recipient countries. This largely involves acceptance of trainees in Japan ❖1, dispatch of experts from Japan to developing countries ❖2, and provision of equipment or materials for the transfer of technologies.

"Project-type technical cooperation" comprehensively and effectively combines all three of the above. For example, Kenya's Jomo Kenyatta University of Agriculture and

ジョモ・ケニヤッタ農工大学は、1978年に日本の無償資金協力によって建設されましたが、その後、継続的に専門家の派遣や研修員の受け入れ、機材供与などを行い、ケニアの農工分野での人材育成に大きく貢献しています。

その他、青年海外協力隊⋄3の派遣事業も技術協力の重要な柱となっています。また、世界各地の自然災害や人災に対し、被災者の救済を目的として救助チームや医療チームなどの国際緊急援助隊を派遣したり、テン

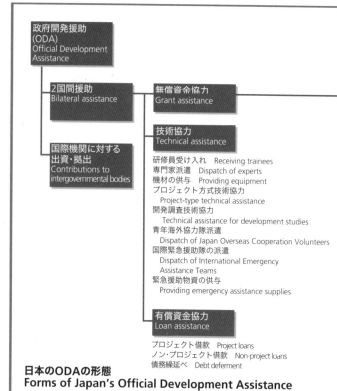

政府開発援助
(ODA)
Official Development
Assistance

2国間援助
Bilateral assistance

無償資金協力
Grant assistance

技術協力
Technical assistance

研修員受け入れ　Receiving trainees
専門家派遣　Dispatch of experts
機材の供与　Providing equipment
プロジェクト方式技術協力
　Project-type technical assistance
開発調査技術協力
　Technical assistance for development studies
青年海外協力隊派遣
　Dispatch of Japan Overseas Cooperation Volunteers
国際緊急援助隊の派遣
　Dispatch of International Emergency
　Assistance Teams
緊急援助物資の供与
　Providing emergency assistance supplies

国際機関に対する
出資・拠出
Contributions to
intergovernmental bodies

有償資金協力
Loan assistance

プロジェクト借款　Project loans
ノン・プロジェクト借款　Non-project loans
債務繰延べ　Debt deferment

日本のODAの形態
Forms of Japan's Official Development Assistance

Technology was built with Japanese grant aid cooperation in 1978, and since that time Japan has continuously sent experts there, hosted trainees, and provided materials, contributing substantially to human resources development in Kenya in the fields of agriculture and industry.

Another important pillar of technical cooperation is the dispatch of Japan Overseas Cooperation Volunteers ❖3. And in response to natural and man-made disasters in various parts of the world, Japan sends International Emergency Assistance Teams, including relief and medical teams, to help

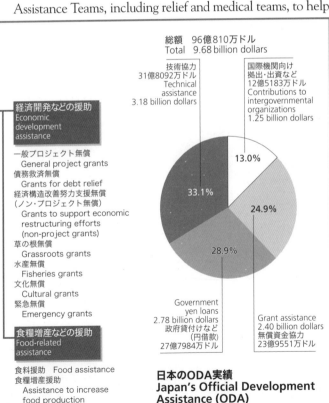

総額　96億810万ドル
Total　9.68 billion dollars

技術協力
31億8092万ドル
Technical
assistance
3.18 billion dollars

国際機関向け
拠出・出資など
12億5183万ドル
Contributions to
intergovernmental
organizations
1.25 billion dollars

経済開発などの援助
Economic
development
assistance

一般プロジェクト無償
　General project grants
債務救済無償
　Grants for debt relief
経済構造改善努力支援無償
（ノン・プロジェクト無償）
　Grants to support economic
　restructuring efforts
　(non-project grants)
草の根無償
　Grassroots grants
水産無償
　Fisheries grants
文化無償
　Cultural grants
緊急無償
　Emergency grants

食糧増産などの援助
Food-related
assistance

食料援助　Food assistance
食糧増産援助
　Assistance to increase
　food production

13.0%

24.9%

33.1%

28.9%

Government
yen loans
2.78 billion dollars
政府貸付けなど
（円借款）
27億7984万ドル

Grant assistance
2.40 billion dollars
無償資金協力
23億9551万ドル

日本のODA実績
**Japan's Official Development
Assistance (ODA)**

ト、毛布などの緊急援助物資の供与を行うことなども実施しています。さらには、経済・社会基盤の整備等の公共的な開発計画策定等、開発途上国の発展に寄与することを目的とする「開発事業調査」等も大きな役割を果たしています。

有償資金協力は、開発途上国に対して金利、返済期間が緩やかな条件で資金を貸し付けるもので、円貨での貸し付けのため、通称「円借款」と呼ばれています。具体的には、国道や港湾施設、発電所、送配電、上下水道など比較的大きな資金需要に対応し、途上国の経済・社会基盤づくりに貢献しています。たとえばタイにおいては、全国の村落の23%が円借款によって電化され、発電設備についてもその15%が円借款で建設されました。

その他、有償資金協力では、借入国の金融機関を通じて、中小企業を含む製造業や農業など、民間部門の発展を促すための開発金融借款(ツーステップ・ローン)も行っています。

注1　研修員受け入れ：途上国の次代を担う有望な研修員を日本に一定期間受け入れ、様々な専門知識や技術を学んでもらう制度。1996年までに世界各国より13万人以上の研修生を受け入れている。

注2　専門家派遣(プロジェクト方式技術協力によるものも含む)：日本から専門技術を持つ人を派遣し、現地での技術移転

victims and makes grants of emergency relief materials like tents and blankets. Japan also plays an important role by carrying out "development work surveys," whose purpose is to contribute to developing countries' progress by assisting with the formulation of governments' development plans for improving economic and social infrastructures.

Loan aid is extended to developing countries with concessional terms of interest and repayment. Because such loans are made in Japanese yen currency, they are commonly called "yen loans." They are made in response to relatively large financial needs, such as the financing of highways and harbor facilities, electric power plants, power transmission lines, or water supply and sewerage systems. In this way, they contribute to developing countries' economic and social infrastructures. In Thailand, for example, yen loans have been responsible for the electrification of 23% of the country's villages, and 15% of the country's power generation facilities were constructed with yen loans.

One type of loan aid is so-called "two-step loans," whereby the borrowing country channels yen loans through local financial institutions which, in turn, make loans to stimulate the private sector including agriculture and medium- and small-size enterprises.

NOTE 1 Acceptance of trainees — This refers to programs in which persons of special ability, who may be expected to contribute to the future progress of developing countries, are invited to spend a certain period of time in Japan learning technical skills or gaining various types of specialized knowledge. Up to 1996, Japan hosted more than 130,000 trainees from countries around the world.

NOTE 2 Dispatch of experts (including those engaged in project-type technical cooperation) — This refers to the sending of persons with specialized skills to assist with technological

を行う事業で、1996年までの累計で、約
4万8000人以上の専門家を派遣した。

注3　青年海外協力隊は、技術と情熱を
持つ日本の青年男女が、開発途上国で現
地の人々と生活を共にしながら経済・社
会の発展に協力するもので、派遣はこれ
まで66ヵ国に1万7000人にものぼる。

青年海外協力隊連絡先
国際協力事業団・青年海外協力隊事務局
〒151–0053
東京都渋谷区代々木2–1–1
新宿マインズタワー　6階
Tel.：03–5352–7261

Q 日本のODAはどんな歴史や理念を持っていますか。

　　第2次世界大戦後、米国や世界銀行など
から経済支援や融資を受け、疲弊した経済
の安定・復興を遂げた日本は※4、1954年
10月にコロンボ・プラン※5に加盟し、政府
ベースによる経済協力(技術協力)を開始し
ました。
　　1960年代前半頃までは、1954年の対ビ
ルマ(現ミャンマー)賠償を皮切りとしたアジ
ア諸国に対する平和条約、賠償・経済協力
協定に基づく戦後賠償が主なものでしたが、
1960年代後半からの高度経済成長による経
済力の伸長により、援助の量的な拡大と技
術協力、有償資金協力(円借款供与)に加え
た無償資金協力の開始など、援助形態の多

transfers in the host countries. Up to 1996, Japan has sent abroad a total of more than 48,000 such experts.

NOTE 3 Japan Overseas Cooperation Volunteers are young Japanese men and women with both skills and enthusiasm who live with people in developing countries, assisting them with various types of economic and social development projects. Up to now, there have been a total of about 17,000 volunteers in 66 countries. Persons who want information on recruitment procedures should contact:

> Japan Overseas Cooperation Volunteers Head Office
> c/o Japan International Cooperation Agency
> Shinjuku Maynds Tower, 6th Floor
> Yoyogi 2–1–1, Shibuya-ku, Tokyo 151–0053
> Phone: 03–5352–7261

Q What are the history and ideals of Japan's ODA?

After the Second World War, Japan received loans and other economic assistance from the United States and the World Bank which helped stabilize and revitalize its weakened economy ❖4. In October 1954, Japan joined the Colombo Plan ❖5, and started economic cooperation (in the form of technical assistance) at the intergovernmental level.

Until the mid-1960s, most of Japan's economic cooperation was in the form of postwar reparations to Asian countries, given first of all to Burma (now called Myanmar) in 1954. It was based upon peace treaties and formal agreements on reparations and economic cooperation. As a result of the increased economic potential which Japan derived from its rapid economic growth since the latter half of the 1960s, the amount of assistance increased greatly, and types of assistance

様化が進みました。1978年から現在に至るまで、5次にわたる中期目標の下に、計画的に政府開発援助が進められています。

援助の内容も経済インフラの整備に加えて、基礎生活分野や人づくりに対する援助の拡充が行われ、対象地域もアジア中心から、中近東、アフリカ、中南米、大洋州地域まで広がりを見せました。1989年には米国を抜き世界最大の援助供与国(トップドナー)となり、以来、1990年を除き世界第1位の援助供与国となっています。

日本の援助は1992年に閣議決定された「政府開発援助大綱(ODA大綱)」において、(1)人道的配慮、(2)開発途上国の安定と発

1950年 1月	コロンボ・プラン発足 Start of Colombo Plan	
1951年 9月	サンフランシスコ講和条約調印	
	Signing of San Francisco Peace Treaty	
1952年 8月	世銀・IMFに加盟 Joining the World Bank and IMF	
1953年	世銀からの第1回借款(発電所)	
	First loan from the World Bank (for electric power plant)	
1954年10月	コロンボ・プランへ加盟 Joining the Colombo Plan	
11月	賠償の開始(ビルマ・現ミャンマー)	
	First reparations payments (to Burma: now Myanmar)	
1956年12月	国際連合へ加盟 Joining the United Nations	
1958年 2月	最初の円借款(インド) First yen loan (to India)	
1961年 3月	海外経済協力基金(OECF)設立 Establishment of OECF	
9月	世銀からの借款(東海道新幹線)	
	Loan from World Bank to build Tōkaidō Shinkansen railway	
1965年 4月	青年海外協力隊(JOCV)設立 Establishment of JOCV	
1966年11月	世銀から最終借款(東京〜静岡間高速道路)	
	Last loan from World Bank (to build Tokyo-Shizuoka Expressway)	

日本の途上国援助の歩み
Important Dates on the Path of Japan's Assistance to Developing Countries

were expanded to include grant aid in addition to technical cooperation and loan aid (i.e., yen loans). Since 1978, Official Development Assistance (ODA) programs have been carried out in accordance with five consecutive medium-term targets.

Sectoral assistance has been expanded to include, in addition to improvements in economic infrastructure, basic human needs and human resources development. Moreover, regions to which this development assistance is given have expanded beyond Asia, where almost all of it was previously concentrated, to the Middle East, Africa, Central and South America, and Oceania. In 1989, Japan surpassed the United States to become the world's top donor and has remained in this position every year since, with the exception of 1990.

According to the ODA Charter adopted by the Cabinet in 1992, Japan's ODA follows these four basic principles: (1) humanitarian considerations; (2) recognition of interdependence

1969年		一般無償資金協力の開始 Start of general grant assistance
1974年	8月	国際協力事業団(JICA)設立 Establishment of JICA
1976年	7月	賠償支払い完了 End of reparations payments
1978年	7月	第1次中期目標発表 Announcement of First Medium-Term Goals
1981年	1月	第2次中期目標設定 Setting of Second Medium-Term Goals
1985年	9月	第3次中期目標設定 Setting of Third Medium-Term Goals
1987年		国際緊急援助隊創設 Establishment of International Emergency Assistance Team
1988年	6月	第4次中期目標設定 Setting of Fourth Medium-Term Goals
1989年		ODA実績DAC諸国中世界一 ODA is largest among DAC donor countries.
1992年	6月	政府開発援助大綱(ODA大綱)閣議決定 Cabinet resolution approves ODA Charter.
1993年	6月	第5次中期目標設定 Setting of Fifth Medium-Term Goals
	10月	第1回アフリカ開発会議 First Africa Development Conference
1994年	2月	地球規模問題 イニシアティブ(人口・エイズ問題) Global Issues Initiative (population and AIDS issues)
1996年	4月	対アフリカ支援イニシアティブ発表 Announcement of Africa Assistance Initiative

展は、世界全体の平和と繁栄にとり不可欠との相互依存性の認識、(3)環境の保全、(4)開発途上国の自助努力支援の4つを基本理念として掲げています。

さらに、(1)環境と開発の両立、(2)援助の軍事的用途および国際紛争助長への使用の回避、(3)開発途上国の軍事支出、大量破壊兵器の開発・製造、武器の輸出入などの動向への注意、(4)開発途上国の民主化の促進、市場指向型経済導入の努力、基本的人権や自由の保障状況への注意を踏まえ、相手国の要請、経済社会状況、2国間関係等を総合的に判断した上で援助が進められています。

注4 東海道新幹線、東名高速道路(東京〜静岡間)は世界銀行からの融資で建設されたもの。

注5 コロンボ・プラン：アジア・太平洋地域の国々の経済・社会開発を促進するため、1950年に発足した国際機関。

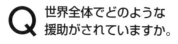

Q 世界全体でどのような援助がされていますか。

1996年における国際機関を含む世界のすべての資金源から開発途上国への資金の流れ(直接投資、銀行貸付等の民間資金を含む)

seen in the fact that the developing countries' stability and development are indispensable to the peace and prosperity of the world as a whole; (3) environmental conservation, and (4) support for self-help efforts on the part of developing countries.

Implementation of Japan's ODA is based on comprehensive consideration of recipient countries' requests, their socioeconomic conditions, and bilateral relations with Japan, as well as the following four points: (1) environmental conservation and development should be pursued in tandem; (2) any use of ODA for military purposes or for aggravation of international conflicts should be avoided; (3) attention should be paid to trends in recipient countries' military expenditures, any development or production of weapons of mass destruction, and arms exports and imports; (4) attention should be paid to efforts for promoting democratization and introduction of a market-oriented economy, and the situation regarding the securing of basic human rights and freedoms in the recipient country.

NOTE 4 For example, the Tōkaidō Shinkansen railway line and a section (between Tokyo and Shizuoka) of the Tōmei Expressway were built with loans from the World Bank.

NOTE 5 The Colombo Plan — This international body was established in 1950 to promote economic and social development in countries of the Asia-Pacific region.

Q In the world as a whole, what sorts of assistance from developed to developing countries are being given?

In 1996, the flow of financial resources (including direct investments, bank loans and other private funds) from all sources, including intergovernmental organizations, into

は、3039億ドルで、このうちODAの総額はその19.2%にあたる582億ドル(対前年比2.5%減)となっています。(DAC❖6主要援助国の96年ODA実績(87ページ参照))。

開発問題に対しては、冷戦構造が崩壊した現在、地球的連帯による取り組みが求められていますが、一方で、先進諸国には景気低迷による資金不足やアフリカ諸国の開発の遅れに対する無力感などもあり、開発援助への消極的な姿勢が見られるのも事実です。

こうした中、我が国は、1993年の東京サミット以来、途上国と先進国がより建設的なパートナーシップをもって開発に取り組むべきとの考え方を提唱してきました。このような考え方は1996年5月のOECD/DACにおいて、採択された新開発戦略❖7にも取り入れられています。また、新開発戦略は同年のリヨン・サミットの経済コミュニケでも歓迎されるなど次第に国際的な理解を得つつあり、1997年のデンバー・サミットにおいては、このような考え方を具体的行動に移していくことが今後の課題とされました。

OECD/DACの新開発戦略においては、具体的な開発目標として、貧困人口の割合の半減や教育の普及、乳幼児死亡率の削減等をかかげ、途上国、先進国双方の努力を求めています。すなわち、先進国においては、援助の実施にあたり、各国のニーズや状況に柔軟に対応して様々な政策措置を組み合わせる「個別的アプローチ」と、政府開発援助

the developing countries amounted to 303.9 billion dollars, of which ODA constituted 19.2% or 58.2 billion dollars, a 2.5% decrease compared with the previous year. (Please refer to the table on p.87 of ODA amounts provided by the major DAC❖6 donor countries in 1996.)

With the collapse of the Cold War structure, a new global approach to development problems, based on the concept of global solidarity, is being sought. The reality, however, is that in many cases attitudes toward development assistance are not as positive as they might be. This observation reflects insufficient funding capacities as a result of economic problems in the developed countries as well as a sense of impotence regarding, for example, many African countries' slowness in progressing toward development goals.

Under these circumstances, since the 1993 Tokyo Summit, Japan has emphasized the need for developing and developed countries to jointly tackle development problems through constructive partnerships. This thinking was included in the New Development Strategy ❖7 adopted by the OECD/DAC in May 1996. This New Development Strategy was welcomed in the economic communiqué of the Lyon Summit later in 1996 and is, in general, winning international recognition. At the 1997 Denver Summit, it was recognized that to translate these ideas into concrete action is essential and will continue to be so in the future.

The new development strategy of the OECD/DAC calls on both the developing and developed countries to make efforts to attain specific development goals, such as cutting in half the percentage of people living in extreme poverty, making opportunities for education universally available, and reducing infant mortality rates. It advocates that the developed countries, in providing assistance, should adopt "individual approaches" bringing together various types of policy measures

のみならず、貿易、民間投資など、開発に関連するあらゆる政策手段を視野に入れて開発を促進する「包括的アプローチ」をとるべきこと、並びに先進国同士の援助調整を図るべきことが指摘されています。

また、開発途上国については、途上国自身が自らの開発の主役であるべきとの「オーナーシップ」の考え方が重視されています。さらに、先進国から途上国へといった従来の援助の図式を超え、発展段階の進んだ途上国が後発の途上国に対し支援を行うといった南南協力の重要性も指摘されています。こうした協力は、発展段階に適合した効果的な技術移転が可能との利点を持っており、益々増大する援助のニーズへの対応の道を広げるものとして期待されています。

注6 DAC；開発援助委員会(Development Assistance Committee)；開発途上国に対する援助の量的・質的改善を目的としたOECDの一委員会。96年末現在日本を含む21ヵ国が加盟。

注7 DAC開発戦略の具体的目標
(1) 貧困人口の割合を半減
 (2015年まで)
(2) すべての国において初等教育を普遍化(2015年まで)
(3) 初等・中等教育における男女格差を解消 (2005年まで)

that respond in a flexible way to the needs of each recipient country. At the same time, they advocate a "comprehensive approach" which promotes development by expanding the field of view to include policy measures related not only to ODA but also to other developmental factors, like trade and private investments. Furthermore, it is advocated that developed countries coordinate among themselves their assistance efforts.

As for the developing countries, emphasis is given to the concept of "ownership," whereby developing countries are encouraged to see themselves as playing the leading role in their own development. Importance is also attached to so-called "South-South cooperation," which, transcending the traditional frameworks of assistance flowing from developed to developing countries, envisages assistance being given by relatively advanced developing countries to those that are still relatively underdeveloped. Such cooperation has the advantage of making possible effective technological transfers suited to specific stages of development, and it is hoped that these nations will widen the avenues of response to ever-growing assistance needs.

NOTE 6 DAC — The Development Assistance Committee, a committee of the OECD, aims at improving the quality and increasing the amount of assistance to developing countries. At the end of 1996 it had 21 member countries, including Japan.

NOTE 7 The specific goals of the DAC development strategy include the following:
(1) reducing by half the proportion of people living in extreme poverty by 2015;
(2) universal primary education in all countries by 2015;
(3) elimination of gender disparity in primary and secondary education by 2005;

(4) 乳児および5歳未満幼児の死亡率を
　　3分の1に低下（2015年まで）

(5) 妊産婦死亡率を4分の1に低下
　　（2015年まで）

(6) 森林、水産資源等に表れる環境破壊
　　の傾向を逆転するなど（2015年まで）

Q 日本も財政赤字が大きな問題になっているのに、なぜ他の国に援助をするんですか。

　日本は、資源小国であり、その経済的繁栄と安全は、平和で安定した国際社会、そして諸外国との友好関係に大きく依存しています。開発途上国への支援や地球規模的問題に対して積極的に取り組んでいくことは、諸外国との友好関係と安定した国際環境を築くことにつながり、ひいては日本自身の平和と繁栄に寄与することになるのです。

　事実、1995年の阪神・淡路大震災の時、世界中からお見舞いや励ましの言葉を受け、76の国・地域、国際機関などから支援の申し出が寄せられました。その中には自国の経済状況も決してゆとりがあるわけでなく、日本が日頃から支援している国も少なくありませんでした。これは政府開発援助を含めて様々な努力によって日本が培ってきた、世界各国の信頼関係のあかしといえます。

　また、過去を振り返れば、現在の日本の経済発展は日本のみによって成し遂げられたのではなく、戦後の苦しい時期に、米国

(4) a reduction by two-thirds in the mortality rate for infants and children under age 5 by 2015;

(5) a reduction by three-fourths in the maternal mortality rate by 2015; and

(6) reversion of the current trends toward deforestation, depletion of marine resources, and other sorts of environmental degradation by 2015.

Q Why does Japan give assistance to other countries when Japan itself has a large fiscal deficit?

Japan is a country of scarce natural resources and its security and economic prosperity are greatly dependent upon a peaceful, stable international society and upon friendly relations with foreign countries. To actively engage in assistance to developing countries and in issues of global scope is essential to the building of good relations with other countries and to a stable international environment. This contributes, in turn, to Japan's own peace and welfare.

At the time of the Hanshin-Awaji Earthquake in 1995, Japan received expressions of sympathy and encouragement from around the world, as well as offers of assistance from 76 countries, regions, and international organizations. Economic conditions in many of these countries were certainly stringent and not a few were countries which had received assistance from Japan. This may be cited as an example of the sorts of relations based upon trust among the countries of the world which Japan has tried to cultivate through various means, including development assistance.

Looking back over the past, Japan's present economic development was achieved not by Japan alone but came about as a result of powerful assistance in the political and

をはじめとする国際社会からの政治・経済面での力強い支援があったからこそ実現したものです。

今日の国際情勢の中で、今や巨大な経済力を持つに至った日本が、自国の繁栄だけを願い、国際社会を無視するというのは益々相互依存関係が深まった今日、不可能なことなのです。積極的なリーダーシップと責任ある行動により、多くの困難に直面している国際社会を支える側に回ることこそが今の日本に求められているのであり、このことが、国際社会において日本の考え方を理解し支持してくれる友人を増やし、最終的に日本の国益、すなわち日本国民の利益を実現していくことにもつながるのです。

Q 日本の援助は国際的に見て少ないのではないですか。

1996年の日本のODA実績は、94億3900万ドルで6年連続世界第1位となりました。しかし、対GNP比では0.2%と、DAC諸国21ヵ国中19位であり、国際目標の0.7%の基準からはまだ低い水準にあるのは確かです。

また、日本のODAは、円借款の規模が大きいことを反映して、贈与の比率は41.4%(95/96年平均)、金利や償還期間等を基に算出される援助の条件の緩やかさの指標であるグラントエレメントは80.5%(95/96年平均)と、いずれもDAC諸国の平均(それぞれ76.9%、91.8%)を下回っています。し

economic spheres that was provided, during the difficult period following the Second World War, by the United States and other members of the international community.

Given international conditions today, when interdependent relationships are becoming ever deeper, it is impossible for Japan, with its giant economic potential, to ignore international society or hope for its own prosperity alone. What is being required of Japan is active leadership and responsible action in supporting and assisting an international society that is facing many difficulties. This will increase the number of friends, around the globe, who understand and support Japan's way of thinking, and it will ultimately contribute to Japan's own national interest, that is to say, the welfare of the Japanese people.

Q Isn't Japan's assistance small compared to that of other countries?

In 1996, the total amount of Japan's ODA was 9.439 billion dollars, ranking for the sixth consecutive year as the largest amount of ODA provided by any single country. This represented 0.2% of Japan's GNP, a proportion that ranked 19th among the 21 DAC member countries. It is true that this level is still low compared to the 0.7% of GNP which is recognized as an international goal.

Reflecting the fact that yen loans constitute a large part of Japan's ODA, the proportion of grant aid within ODA was an average of 41.4% over the two-year period 1995-96, compared to a 76.9% average among all DAC members during the same period. The "grant element" in Japan's yen loans during the same two-year period was 80.5%, compared to a 91.8% average among all bilateral loans by DAC members. This index indicates the

形態 Form	1996年	構成比 %
I 公的開発資金（ODF） Official development funding	69.5	22.6
1. 政府開発援助（ODA） Official development assistance	57.7	18.8
A. 2国間支出 Bilateral expenditures	35.4	11.5
B. 国際機関による支出 Expenditures through international bodies	22.3	7.3
2. その他ODF Other official development funding	11.8	3.8
A. 2国間支出 Bilateral expenditures	7.9	2.6
B. 国際機関による支出 Expenditures through international bodies	3.9	1.3
II 輸出信用総額 Export credit total	3.5	1.1
うち、短期 (Short-term)	0.5	0.2
III 民間資金（PF）Private funding	234.0	76.2
1. 直接投資（OECD諸国） Direct investments (OECD countries)	60.0	19.5
うち、オフ・ショアーセンター (Offshore centers)	5.0	1.6
2. 国際的銀行貸付 International bank loans	70.0	22.8
うち、短期 (Short-term)	50.0	16.3
3. 債券貸付総額 Loan bond total	86.0	28.0
4. その他民間資金 Other private funding	12.0	3.9
5. NGOによる贈与 Grants by NGOs	6.0	2.0
全資金フロー（I+II+III） Total flow of funds（I+II+III）	307.0	100%

単位：10億ドル　出典：97年DACプレス・リリース
Unit: billions of dollars　Source: 1997 DAC Press Releases

全資金ソースからの途上国への資金の流れ
Flows of Monetary Assistance to Developing Countries (from all sources)

たがって、今後、全体の援助量の拡大のみならず、贈与（無償資金協力、技術協力）の拡充や、対後発開発途上国援助の無償化のさらなる推進も課題となっています。

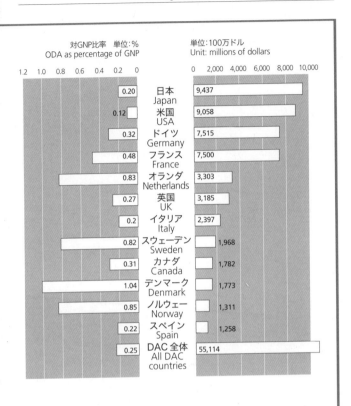

主要DAC諸国の1996年ODA実績
ODA from Major DAC Countries in 1996

"softness" of financial terms and is determined by interest rates, repayment schedules, and other factors. Tasks for the future will thus include not merely expanding the amount of total assistance but expanding the proportion of grants-in-aid (i.e., grant aid cooperation and technical cooperation) and further promoting grant assistance, particularly to the least developed countries (LDC).

Q 日本の援助は、日本の企業が
儲けるためにあるのではないのですか。

　　援助が自国企業のためのいわゆる「ひもつ
き」であるかどうかをみるための指標として
アンタイド率❖8 というものがあります。日
本の2国間援助のアンタイド率は1995年で
は82.1%(96年の円借款のアンタイド率は
100%)で、これは主要援助国間でも極めて高
い水準です。したがって、我が国のODAが
「ひもつき」、日本企業の「輸出振興策」であ
るなど、日本の企業が儲けるためにあるとの
考えはまったくの誤りです。

注8　アンタイド率：2国間のODAでは、
あるプロジェクトなどの援助に必要な資
材や役務(工事などの従事者)の調達先を、
援助する側の国などに限定することをタ
イドと言い、そうした調達先を限定しな
いことを一般にアンタイドと呼び、アン
タイドの案件が全体に占める割合をアン
タイド率という。

Q 日本は、援助される側の意向を
十分踏まえて援助を行っていないのでは
ないですか。

　　開発途上国に対する協力は、援助国側か
らの一方的な押しつけや、逆に途上国からの
要請のみを主体とした受動的なものでは十分
な効果を期待できません。その意味で、途上
国への協力は援助国と被援助国との共同作
業であり、両者の十分な考え方や意見の調

Q Isn't Japan's assistance given to make profits for Japanese companies?

The "untied rate"❖8 is an indicator showing the extent to which assistance is tied to the advantage of companies in the donor country. Japan's untied rate for bilateral assistance in 1995 was 82.1%, and its untied rate for yen loans was 100% in 1996, higher figures than in most other major donor countries. Thus it is erroneous to think that Japan's ODA is usually "tied" or that it is a policy designed mainly to promote exports by Japanese companies.

NOTE 8 Untied rate — In the case of bilateral ODA, assistance for a given project is said to be "tied" if it is specified that necessary materials or personnel (such as construction workers) must be procured only from the country providing the assistance. When such conditions are not specified, the assistance is generally called "untied." The "untied rate" is the percentage of total ODA funds allocated to "untied" projects.

Q Doesn't Japan often extend assistance without paying due attention to the views of recipient countries?

It cannot be expected that cooperation with developing countries will be fully effective if there is unilateral imposition of ideas or methods by donor countries, or conversely, if donor countries provide the assistance too passively, taking into account only what developing countries request. In this sense, cooperative efforts with developing countries must be joint

整を踏まえたものである必要があります。こうした考えの下に日本は、途上国と援助に関する様々なレベルでの政策対話を重視し実施しています。

具体的にはハイレベルの政府要人の往来の機会をとらえての対話、中・長期的視点から総合的な政策対話を行う経済協力総合調査団の派遣、援助の形態別の政策対話のための調査団の派遣や年次協議の実施などです。こうした政策対話や調査を通じ、国別の現状、開発計画、経済政策、および2国間関係を踏まえた援助方針を決定し、協力案件の選定を行うなど、援助の効果的かつ効率的実施に努めています。

被援助国民の一部しか援助の恩恵にあずかっていないとの報道がありますが。

日本は援助を実施する際に事前に開発途上国と十分な政策協議をかさねると共に、綿密な調査を行い、対象となるプロジェクトの国家開発計画の中での優先度や、国民一般にもたらす経済的効果を十分考慮した上で協力を実施しています。

たとえば、日本の無償資金協力の1つである「草の根無償資金協力」は、被援助国民の中でも今まで援助が行き届きにくかった

endeavors of the assisted and the assisting parties, and must be undertaken after due coordination of opinions and views. It is with this intent that Japan gives great attention to assistance-related policy dialogues, at many levels, with developing countries.

More specifically, these policy dialogues include those at the highest level occasioned by visits to Japan, and vice-versa, of top government officials, as well as the dispatch of Survey Missions for Economic Cooperation which undertake wide-ranging policy discussions with medium-term and long-term perspectives. Japan dispatches other survey teams for policy dialogues on specific types of assistance projects and holds annual consultation meetings. Through such policy dialogues and studies, Japan sets assistance guidelines and chooses cooperation projects after taking into account specific conditions in different countries, these countries' development planning and economic policies, and overall bilateral relations. In this way, Japan tries to makes its assistance both efficient and effective.

Q What about reports that only some of the people in recipient countries benefit from ODA?

Before deciding to undertake an economic cooperation project, Japan holds adequate policy consultations with the country concerned and makes careful studies of the proposal. Due attention is given to the priority that the project has within the recipient country's national development plans, and to the economic results which may be expected for the country's people as a whole.

For example, a type of Japanese grant aid, so-called "grassroots grant aid," though small in amount, directly reaches population strata and geographical areas of recipient

アンタイド Untied
タイド Tied
部分アンタイド Partly untied

単位:%　約束額ベース1994年
Percentages of commitments for 1994

DAC議長報告より算出
Source: Reports from the DAC Chairman

**主要DAC諸国の2国間ODAの
アンタイド比率
Untied Rates of Bilateral ODA
from Major DAC Countries**

日本 Japan
フランス France
オランダ Netherlands
カナダ Canada
米国 USA
英国 UK
イタリア Italy

層・地域に対し、少額ではあるが、直接、そしてすぐに役立つ援助を行うものであり、近年、特に高い評価を得ています。

また、ダムや発電所、道路といった「経済インフラ」に対する援助は、ともすれば被援助国民の一部にしか恩恵をもたらさないと考えがちです。しかし、これらを通じた産業の振興は、結果的にはその被援助国の経済成長を通じて社会全体の底上げをもたらし、国民1人1人の生活水準を改善するものなのです。

さらに日本は、実施したプロジェクトがその後もきちんと管理・運営されているか、効果があがっているかをチェックするため、内外の有識者や民間団体に委託したり、他の援助国や機関と合同で行うなどの方法で、実施済み案件の事後評価を実施していますが、その報告のほとんどは、日本の援助が開発途上国の多くの国民の役に立っていると指摘しています。もっとも例年40ヵ国で120～150件前後実施されているこうした評価の報告書の中には、問題点や改善すべき点について指摘があることもありますので、政府はこうした問題点等についても率直に公表するととも

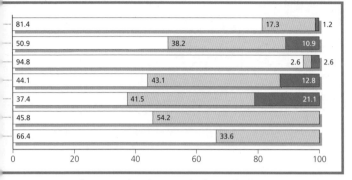

countries that were hard to reach through previous assistance efforts. This assistance has in recent years received a particularly high reputation.

There is a tendency to think that assistance for so-called "economic infrastructure," such as dams, electric power plants and roads, brings benefits to only a limited stratum of a recipient country's population. However, the resulting stimulus provided to local industries will ultimately, through the processes of economic growth in the recipient country, pull the whole society upward, improving living standards for everybody.

In order to check up on whether a project which has already been implemented is being well managed with positive results, Japan carries out follow-up evaluations which are commissioned out to knowledgeable Japanese or foreign individuals or NGOs, or conducted in cooperation with other donor countries and international aid organizations. Almost all these reports indicate that Japan's assistance indeed benefits a very large portion of the people in the recipient countries. Of course, among these 120 to 150 evaluation reports on some 40 countries that are produced every year, certain problem areas and matters that need improvement are pointed out. The Japanese government makes these problems public, and makes efforts to carry out appropriate follow-up

に、適切なフォローアップに努めることとしています。

Q 世界の開発問題に携わっている 日本のNGOにはどんなところがありますか。

日本における開発協力関係のNGO❖9は約300団体あると言われており、開発途上国における医療、保健衛生、人材育成、地域産業向上、女性自立支援、民間物資輸送などの分野でプロジェクトを実施しています。

この中で診療所・医療センターの建設や医師、看護婦の派遣等を内容とした医療事業が依然として大きな割合を占めていますが、これに人材育成事業、地域産業向上事業が次いでいます。

人材育成事業では、学校・図書館の建設や専門家および指導員の派遣を通じ、開発途上国において次世代を担う子供たちの健全な育成や、地域の発展に貢献する人材の育成が図られています。

日本のNGOの活動地域としては歴史的、地理的な関係もありアジア諸国が中心ですが、近年、活動の活発化とともにアフリカ等の他の地域への関心も高まっています。しかし、日本のNGOは、開発協力を推進する意欲を持ちながらも、その財政基盤が十分確立されていないことなどから、欧州諸国のNGOに比べてその規模、活動は残念ながら限られたものとなっているのが現状です。国

activities.

Q What sorts of Japanese NGOs deal with global development problems?

Is is reported that in Japan there are approximately 300 NGOs ❖9 whose work has to do with assisting development efforts. They are carrying out projects in developing countries in such fields as medical care, public health and hygiene, human resources development, improvement of local industries, support for women's self-help projects and the privately-managed transport of goods and materials.

Among these projects, health care projects, such as the construction of health centers and the sending of doctors and nurses from Japan, account for the largest portion of aid efforts, followed by projects for human resources development and the improvement of local industries.

In human resources development, through the construction of schools and libraries and the dispatch of experts and consultants, efforts are being made to contribute to the wholesome education of the children who will determine the course of the next generation and to develop persons who can contribute to the development of local regions and rural areas.

Japanese NGOs are most active in Asian countries which have historical and geographical links with Japan. However, in recent years there has been increasing interest in Africa and other areas of the world. While Japanese NGOs want to promote development cooperation, their scale and activities are unfortunately rather limited owing to their inadequate financial base in comparison with NGOs based in European countries. In 1995, levels of NGO assistance, on a per capita basis, were over 30 dollars in Switzerland, the

民1人あたりのNGO援助実績(1995年)は、スイス、オランダ、ルクセンブルクが30ドル以上、米国が約10ドル、ドイツが約14ドルに比し、日本は3.8ドルにとどまっています(DAC平均は8.6ドル)。

注9 NGO:「非政府組織(Non-Governmental Organization)」の略。営利団体や政党などを除く民間組織。日本では1970年代に海外の自然災害や難民に対する救援を目的に結成されたのが始まり。80年代にかけてインドシナ難民やアフリカ飢餓などをきっかけに飛躍的に増えた。

Q 草の根レベルでの日本のNGO活動に対する
政府からの支援はあるのですか。

　日本のNGOが開発途上国で行う開発協力活動に対し、その事業費の一部を補助する制度として外務省によるNGO事業補助金制度があります。これは総事業費の2分の1以下を援助(ただし1500万円程度を限度)するもので、1996年度の交付実績は8億1700万円でした。

　また、近年国際ボランティア活動に従事する者が海外での災害や事故等に遭遇するケースが増加しており、こうした場合の措置への対応策として、NGO事業補助金制度の中に、これらボランティアの海外旅行傷害保険料および戦争特約保険料の一部を補助する国際ボランティア補償支援制度があります。

Netherlands and Luxembourg, about 14 dollars in Germany, about 10 dollars in the United States, but only 3.8 dollars in Japan. The average for the DAC member countries was 8.6 dollars.

NOTE 9 NGO — This is the abbreviation of "nongovernmental organization." NGOs are private groups and do not include profit-making organizations or political parties. In Japan, the first NGOs were organized in the 1970s to aid refugees and victims of natural disasters overseas. During the 1980s, the number grew dramatically in response to Indochinese refugees and to famine in Africa.

Q Is there any government support for the activities of Japanese NGOs at the grassroots level?

The Ministry of Foreign Affairs has a system of subsidies for NGO activities whereby a part of the expenditures made by Japanese NGOs for development cooperation activities in developing countries is covered. These subsidies are limited to half of total expenditures (no more than around 15 million yen). During fiscal 1996, the total amount of government money allocated under this system was 817 million yen.

Given that in recent years there has been growth in the number of cases where people engaged in international volunteer activities have encountered accidents or disasters abroad, the Japanese government, within its system of subsidies for NGO activities, provides expenditures covering a part of the costs of NGO volunteers' overseas travel and accident insurance, as well as special insurance against material losses

NGO事業補助金と並んで国民参加型援助を推進するものとして草の根無償資金協力があります。これは、開発途上国の地方公共団体、研究・医療機関および途上国で活動するNGOなどが実施する比較的小規模なプロジェクトに対し、日本の在外公館が中心となって無償で資金協力(1件あたりの規模は数十万円から1000万円程度)をするものです。日本のNGOについても現地に根付いた活動を行っている場合は支援の対象となります。

対象事業としては、NGOが途上国で行う草の根レベルでの開発協力プロジェクトの経費で、主に施設建設、資機材購入、セミナー開催等の経費が対象となります。申請は在外公館で受けつけています。ただし、同一案件に対し、上記NGO事業補助金との二重の申請はできません。

Q 地方自治体が行う援助活動に対して、国はどのような支援をしていますか。

途上国の開発・自立の基盤となる「人づくり」は従来より日本の援助の重点分野で、特に、地方自治体がそれぞれの地域の特性や幅広いノウハウを生かして行う途上国への専門家派遣や研修員受け入れ等の国際協力事業は、途上国におけるきめ細かい「人づくり」、さらに日本の地方の国際化に役立って

or casualties in areas of potential warfare.

Besides the subsidies for NGO activities, another mechanism to promote assistance projects of a type in which ordinary people participate is so-called "grassroots grant aid." This involves grants of financial assistance (from several hundred thousand to 10 million yen per project) given through Japanese embassies and consulates for relatively small-scale projects undertaken by Japanese NGOs or other groups in developing countries, such as research or medical organizations or, in some cases, local public entities.

These grants are provided to cover costs of grassroots level development cooperation projects in which NGOs participate and include mainly costs associated with the construction of various facilities, the purchase of goods or equipment, or the sponsoring of seminars. Applications for such assistance are made through Japanese government offices abroad. For any given project, a double application for subsidies through the earlier mentioned subsidy program is not permitted.

Q What sorts of support does the Japanese government give to overseas assistance activities carried out by Japanese local governments?

Traditionally, a priority field for Japanese overseas assistance has been "human resources development" to help in building the foundations for developing countries' progress and self-sufficiency. In particular, international cooperation activities carried out by local governments (e.g., the hosting of trainees from overseas and the sending of experts to developing countries) are ways in which these Japanese local gov-

います。

　こうした中、外務省は地方自治体が行う
途上国からの研修員受け入れ事業、専門家
派遣事業、留学生受け入れ事業などに対し
て補助金を交付しています。
　また、地方自治体の国際協力に対して
は、国際協力事業団(JICA)を通じた支援
や共同事業も展開されています。ODA事
業や途上国の開発ニーズに関する情報提供
をはじめ、地方自治体の国際協力業務担当
者を対象に「国際協力実務研修」を実施
し、国際協力の理念、実務知識などの講義
や語学研修を行っています。また、JICA
による途上国研修コースを地方自治体と連
携で行った例も1996年度には159コース
にのぼっています。

Q 特殊技能を身につけていない人でも
携わることができる
援助活動はありますか。

　ボランティア活動の推進、支援を目的に全
国の3分の2の市区町村の社会福祉協議会が
設置するボランティアセンターでは、相談員
やボランティア・コーディネーターが相談に
応じて、ボランティア活動に関する情報提供

ernments can take advantage of their regions' special characteristics and a wide range of know-how. Such activities can contribute much to the great variety of needs for human resources development in developing countries and can at the same time contribute to the "internationalization" of Japan's local areas.

The Ministry of Foreign Affairs provides subsidies for local governments' accepting students and trainees and sending experts abroad.

Support for local governments' international cooperation projects is also given by the Japan International Cooperation Agency (JICA), which may in some cases take part in joint projects. In addition to providing information on ODA projects and developing countries' specific needs, JICA carries out International Cooperation Practical Training Courses for persons in local governments entrusted with the management of international cooperation projects. These courses include language training and lectures on concepts and ideals, as well as specific practical knowledge pertaining to international cooperation activities. In fiscal 1996, the JICA sponsored 159 such courses in cooperation with local governments.

Q Are there any activities related to overseas assistance that even people who lack special skills can take part in?

Two-thirds of the Social Welfare Councils in Japan's cities, wards, towns, and villages have established Volunteer Centers to encourage and support volunteer activities. At these centers, consultants and volunteer coordinators are available to give advice to interested citizens, to provide informa-

や体験活動の実施、ボランティアスクールの開催等の活動のきっかけづくりをしているので、初めて活動をしようとする方はその利用を勧めます。

また、特殊技能がなくとも1人で始められる活動としては、使用済み切手や使用済みプリペイドカードなどを収集・換金し活動資金としているボランティア団体の収集活動への協力や、ボランティア団体および推進機関が実施している募金活動への協力があります。これらに協力するにあたっては、収集ないし募金団体の活動目的、活動内容をよく聞き納得した上で参加することが望ましいです。

また、郵政省では郵便局を窓口に、通常貯金利子の20%以上の任意の額を寄付することにより、NGOを通じて開発途上地域の人々の福祉の向上に役立てる国際ボランティア貯金を実施しています。

その他、開発途上国の子供たちへ学資などの金銭的援助を行い、文通を通じて子供たちの成長と交流を目指す、教育(精神)里親活動というものもあり、個人やグループでの参加が可能です。詳細はボランティアセンター等に問い合わせてください。

tion on volunteer activities, and to facilitate opportunities to participate in activities held at Volunteer Schools or to gain direct experience with volunteer work. We suggest that persons wishing to take part in such activities for the first time make use of these Volunteer Centers.

One type of activity that individuals with no special skills can begin with is to cooperate with fund-raising activities carried out by volunteer organizations and their support groups. One type of fund-raising is to help collect used stamps and used prepaid cards which can be sold to hobby shops for money to support volunteer activities. Before you decide to take part in such collecting or fund-raising activities for a given organization, it is advisable to become well-informed about, and to be sure you agree with, the purposes and details of the organization's work.

Through the intermediary of Japan's post offices, the Ministry of Posts and Telecommunications administers a system of Postal Savings for International Voluntary Aid whereby an amount of 20% or more (to be designated by the account holder) of interest accruing to ordinary postal savings accounts can be designated as a contribution to an NGO of the account holder's choice, to be used to improve the welfare of people in developing areas outside Japan.

There are also so-called "education foster parent" activities whose purpose is to give monetary assistance to children in developing countries for school expenses while promoting, via exchanges of letters, these children's personal growth and at the same time promoting friendship and cultural exchange. One may participate as an individual or as part of a group. For more detailed information, please consult one of the Volunteer Centers.

Q 援助についてもっと詳しく知りたい時は、どこに聞けばいいのですか?

　　援助に対する国民の支持と理解を得るためにも、援助に関する情報を広く国民の方々に提供していくことは最も重要なことの1つと言えます。政府はじめ援助実施機関は、こうした認識に立って、各種刊行物の出版を含む多様な媒体を通じて積極的な情報提供を行っています。

　　また、1993年10月、国際協力に関する情報の窓口として、外務省の協力により「国際協力プラザ」✧10が東京にオープンしました。ここでは、援助や国際協力に関する図書資料、ビデオやCDなどの視聴覚教材、日本の援助プロジェクトの概要や報道記事、受注企業名リストなど種々の資料・情報を整備して広く公開しています。さらに、同プラザでは援助に関する様々な質問・相談に応じているほか、国際協力にかかわるNGOの情報も得ることができます。

注10　国際協力プラザ

〒106–0047

東京都港区南麻布5–2–32

第32興和ビル　1階

TEL. 03–5423–0561

FAX. 03–5423–0564

ホームページ：

http://www.apic.or.jp/plaza/

開館時間：

月〜金10:00–18:00　土10:00–15:00

（日・祝祭日　休館）

Q Where should I inquire if I want to know more about ODA?

To gain the Japanese people's understanding of ODA and support for it, one of the most important things we can do is to make available, as widely as possible, information about it. In this spirit, the Japanese government and various assistance-implementing bodies are actively engaged in providing such information through publications and other means.

As one means of making information on economic cooperation available to the general public, the International Cooperation Plaza ❖10 was opened in Tokyo in October 1993 with the support and under the direction of the Ministry of Foreign Affairs. The Plaza brings together, and makes easily available to the public, various materials and information on ODA and international cooperation, including books and journals, audiovisual materials like videos and CDs, and published outlines and news reports concerning Japan's assistance projects, as well as lists of business enterprises that have received contracts to take part in such projects. At the Plaza, visitors can ask questions and consult about ODA, and they can also receive information about NGOs engaged in international cooperation activities.

NOTE 10

The International Cooperation Plaza is located at this address:

No. 32 Kōwa Building, 1st Floor

Minami Azabu 5–2–32, Minato-ku, Tokyo 106–0047

Phone: 03–5423–0561

Fax: 03–5423–0564

Internet Homepage:

http://www.apic.or.jp/plaza/

Open Monday–Friday 10:00–18:00; Saturday 10:00–15:00

(closed Sundays and holidays)

124

人物紹介

**青年
海外協力隊員**
あさ ひ な ゆたか
朝比奈裕

Asahina
Yutaka
**Japan
Overseas
Cooperation
Volunteer**

パラグアイで
音楽を
教える

　朝比奈さんの人生を変えたのは、1993年、偶然、新宿の書店で見た「青年海外協力隊隊員募集」のポスターでした。当時、彼は大学院で社会科教育を研究していたのですが、「自分の将来はこれでいいのかな、もっと自分がやりたいことがあるのでは——」という漠然とした疑問を感じていたときでもありました。

　自分を変えるチャンスかもしれない——と思った彼は、応募してみることを決心しました。そして、十数倍の競争をくぐり抜けて、彼は隊員に選ばれたのです。

　彼の派遣先はパラグアイに決まりました。パラグアイは南米大陸の中央部にある内陸国で、国民の97％は、先住民のグアラニー族と征服者であったスペイン人とのいわゆる混血です。農業国として発展をしていますが、教育の態勢は遅れていて、特に、情操教育を強化するために、音楽や美術の教育の指導者の派遣が求められていました。

　そこで、彼は音楽の先生としてパラグアイに向かうことになったのです。実は、彼は音楽の専門家ではありません。しかし、以前から合唱団に入っていて、音楽についての十分な知識を持っていました。

　青年海外協力隊の訓練所で2ヵ月半の基礎的な訓練、そして、メキシコでのスペイン語の特訓の後、朝比奈さんはパラグアイの

Teaching Music in Paraguay

What changed Mr. Asahina's life was a poster announcing a campaign to recruit Japan Overseas Cooperation Volunteers (JOCV) which he chanced to see in a Shinjuku bookstore in 1993. At that time he was studying social studies education in a certain graduate school and was feeling a vague question about his future: "Is this what I really want to do from now on, or is there something more I want to accomplish?"

Thinking this could be a chance to change himself, he decided to apply. Making it through the competition—there were about ten times more applicants than available positions—he was chosen as a volunteer.

It was decided that he would go to Paraguay, a country in the center of South America where 97% of the population are so-called mixed-blood descendants of the indigenous Guaraní ethnic group and the Spaniards who once conquered them. While Paraguay is making progress as an agricultural country, improvement is needed in education. To help cultivate the people's esthetic appreciation, teachers were being invited from abroad to give instruction in music and the fine arts.

Mr. Asahina went to Paraguay to teach music. To tell the truth, he was not a music specialist. But he had been a member of a choral society and he had a good deal of knowledge about music in general.

After two and a half months of training at the JOCV Training Center and in a special Spanish-language training course in Mexico, Mr. Asahina went to work at a teacher-

人物紹介

エウセビオ・アジャラ(Eusebio Ayala)という市の教員養成校に赴任しました。つまり、彼は、小学校の先生になるパラグアイの人たちに、音楽を教える先生になったのです。

スペイン語の特訓を受けたとはいえ、最初のうちは、音楽の基礎的な理論、歴史、楽譜の読み方などを正確に伝えるのは困難で、ペアのパラグアイの先生と一緒の授業でしたが、毎日、必死に教えている間に、彼のスペイン語も急速に上達して、やがて、1人で授業を進めることができるようになりました。

音楽の実技の指導になると、合唱できたえた彼の実力が発揮されました。それに、そもそも陽気な気質のパラグアイの人たちです。すぐにリズムにのって盛り上がり、音楽の授業は盛況でした。

あっという間に2年が過ぎ、彼はさらにもう1年、活動期間を延ばし、結局、1996年までの3年間をパラグアイで、音楽の先生として過ごすことになりました。

朝比奈さんと同様に、世界のいたるところに、理科、数学、美術など、様々な知識を教えている隊員たちがいます。開発途上の国々の文化や教育の発展に協力するのが、青年海外協力隊の活動の大きな役割の1つです。

Mr. Asahina and future Paraguayan teachers in a music class

training school in the town of Eusebio Ayala, Paraguay. He became a music teacher for Paraguayans who were studying to be elementary school teachers.

Though he had completed the special training course in Spanish, at first it was difficult to accurately explain basic music theory and history or how to read music notation, so he taught together with a Paraguayan colleague. But working hard every day, his Spanish quickly improved and before long he could handle the lessons by himself.

For giving guidance in practical techniques, the skills he had learned in the choral society stood him in good stead. Then too, his pupils were Paraguayans and their cheerful temperament preconditioned them to join eagerly in making music. So the class was a great success.

Before he knew it, two years passed and he extended the period of his activity for another year. By 1996 he had spent three years teaching music in Paraguay.

Like Mr. Asahina, there are other Japanese Overseas Cooperation Volunteers in places around the world who are teaching science, mathematics, art, and other types of skills and knowledge. Their activities play an important role in working together for developing countries' cultural and educational progress.

地球環境を
護るために
Protecting
the Global Environment

IV

Chapter

Q 地球が温暖化すると何が問題なのですか。
それを防ぐにはどうすればよいのですか。

　　　　地球が温暖化すると、まず考えられるこ
とは、海水の熱膨張や氷河の融解等により
海面が上昇することです。科学者たちの推
定によれば2100年には現在より50cm程度
海面が上昇するそうです。そうなれば南太
平洋に浮かぶ島国などの場合は、国の大部
分が水没するおそれがあります。また、生
物の分布や生態系、農業にも大きな影響を
もたらすと考えられます。

　　　　今後何の対策も講じられない場合、一部
の植物は温暖化の進展に伴う気候変化につ

▶ With his ice statue of a penguin, a member of a Korean NGO sits in front of the entrance to the 1997 Kyoto Conference on Climate Change appealing for measures to prevent global warming.

ペンギンが
溶けている!!
Penguins Are Melting

Q Why is it a problem if the Earth becomes warmer? What can we do to prevent it?

If the Earth should become warmer, one of the first things we might expect to see is a rise in the sea level caused by heat expansion, the melting of glaciers, and so forth. According to estimates by scientists, the ocean surface is likely to rise by about 50 centimeters between now and the year 2100. If that happens, there is the fear that, in the case of some island countries in the South Pacific and elsewhere, large parts of some countries could go under water. It is thought that global warming would also have a profound effect on ecology and the distribution of living organisms as well as on agriculture.

There is the fear that, if no countermeasures are taken, some plant species would be unable to adapt to climate changes

いていけず、絶滅するおそれがあります。また、日射病・熱射病のように直接人体に顕れる悪影響の他、病原体や害虫・害獣の被害が増大する可能性もあります。

地球が温暖化している一番大きな理由は、二酸化炭素(CO_2)やメタン、フロン等(ひとまとめにして温室効果ガスと呼ばれる)の大気中の濃度が増えることにより、本来ならば宇宙に逃げ出して行くべき熱が大気中で吸収されてしまうことにあります。従って、地球温暖化を防ぐためには大気中の温室効果ガス、特にエネルギー消費に伴い大量に発生するCO_2の排出を削減し、また、既に大気中にあるCO_2を除去する方策を考えなければなりません。

CO_2の排出を減らすためには生活のあらゆる場面において省エネルギーなどを推進し、エネルギー消費量を抑制する必要があります。また、光合成によってCO_2を固定化してくれる森林を保護・育成することも重要です。

1992年リオデジャネイロで開催された地球サミットでは地球温暖化問題に対処するための、「気候変動に関する国際連合枠組条約」が採択されました。この条約では、気候系に危険な人為的影響を与えることとならない水準において大気中の温室効果ガスの濃度を安定化させることを究極的な目的としています。

日本では、既に1990年には「地球温暖化防止行動計画」を策定して地球温暖化対策を計画的・総合的に推進していくための方針と取り組むべき対策の全体像を明確にし

accompanying global warming and would become extinct. Besides directly harmful effects on the human body in the form of sunstroke, heatstroke, etc., there is the possibility of an increase in harm brought on by disease-causing bacteria and certain types of harmful insects and animals.

The most important cause of global warming is growing concentrations carbon dioxide (CO_2) and other gases (methane, chlorofluorocarbons, etc.) in the atmosphere, which are known collectively as "greenhouse gases." As the result of growing concentrations of these gases, heat from the sun, which would otherwise discharge into space, is kept within the atmosphere and not allowed to escape. Therefore, in order to prevent global warming, we need to come up with measures to reduce emissions of greenhouse gases, especially CO_2, which humans produce in large quantities as a consequence of large-scale energy consumption. We also need to take up measures that would remove some of the CO_2 already in the atmosphere.

To reduce CO_2 emissions, it will be necessary to restrict energy consumption and promote energy saving and efficiency in various aspects of our lives. It is also important to protect and expand areas covered by forests, which absorb large amounts of CO_2 in the photosynthesis process.

At the Earth Summit held in Rio de Janeiro in 1992, the United Nations Framework Convention on Climate Change was adopted to cope with the global warming issue. This international agreement ultimately aims to stabilize the atmospheric concentration of greenhouse gases at levels which would not result in dangerous, man-made effects on climatic systems.

In 1990, Japan put forward an Action Plan to Prevent Global Warming, which clearly indicated, in a comprehensive and systematic way, policies and measures to prevent global warming. At the 1997 Special Session of the UN

ているほか、開発途上国におけるエネルギー問題に貢献するため1997年の国連環境開発特別総会においてグリーン・イニシアティブを発表しました。

また、日本は地球温暖化防止京都会議(COP3：1997年12月、於京都)の議長国として、21世紀を見据えた地球温暖化防止対策の強化に大きく貢献しています。

Q 酸性雨の被害の現状は
どのようになっていますか。
日本の取り組みはどのようなものですか。

酸性雨は、主に化石燃料(石炭、石油)の燃焼などに伴って生じる硫黄酸化物(SO_x)や窒素酸化物(NO_x)が大気中で種々の化学反応を起こし、大気中のちりの粒子が強い酸性になることにより生じます。そして雨滴が粒子につき、酸性雨として地上に降ってきます。

酸性雨の被害として、ヨーロッパでは既に次のような被害が報告されています。
(1) 湖沼、河川が酸性化され魚類が死滅する。
(2) 土壌の酸化によって樹木が枯れる。
(3) 大理石の建造物が浸食される。

日本では日本海側の森林に枯死が目立つとの報告がありますが、酸性雨が降っていること自体は事実です。

日本の場合は大気汚染防止の観点から既に厳しい環境規制が導入されており、電力業

General Assembly on Environment and Development, Japan announced its "Green Initiative" for contributing to dealing with energy problems in developing countries.

In December 1997, Japan hosted and chaired the Third Session of the Conference of the Parties to the United Nations Framework Convention on Climate Change (COP3), and continues to make important contributions to strengthening countermeasures in the 21st century.

Q What is the present degree of harm being caused by "acid rain"? And how is Japan coping with this issue?

Acid rain results from the process whereby sulfur oxides (SO_x) and nitrogen oxides (NO_x) released into the atmosphere, mainly as a result of the burning of fossil fuels (coal and oil), undergo various chemical reactions in the atmosphere that cause atmospheric dust particles to become strongly acidic. Rain droplets then form around these particles and fall to the ground as acid rain.

The following harmful effects of acid rain have been reported in Europe:
(1) fish dying because of the acidification of marshes and rivers;
(2) trees dying because of soil acidification;
(3) corrosive effects on buildings and other objects made of marble.

In Japan there are frequent reports of trees dying in forests near the Sea of Japan, and it has been established that acid rain is especially common in these areas.

Very strict environmental regulations aimed at preventing atmospheric pollution have been introduced in

界などを中心にSO_xやNO_xの排出量が世界
的に見て極めて低く押さえられています。

Q 日本人の生活は、地球と世界の 環境・自然にどのように結びついていますか。

地球規模の環境問題は相互に密接に関連
しており、私たちが気付かないうちに日本人
の生活も世界の環境・自然に大きな影響を
与えています。

資源に乏しく、輸出入に頼らなければ経済
を維持できない日本にとって、貿易の発達が
環境に与える影響も真剣に考える必要があ

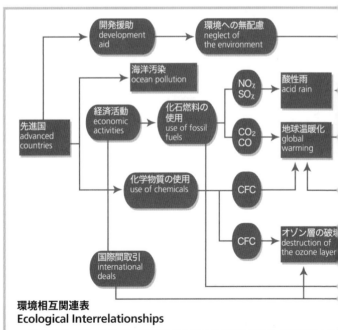

環境相互関連表
Ecological Interrelationships

Japan, and levels of SO$_x$ and NO$_x$ emissions by the electric power industry, etc., have been kept very low compared to most other parts of the world.

Q How is the Japanese people's way of living linked to the Earth's natural environment?

Environmental issues of global scale are closely linked with one another, and the way of life of the Japanese people has affected nature and the world's environment in ways that we may not be aware of.

It is necessary for Japan, which is poor in natural resources and cannot maintain its economy without relying on imports and exports, to think seriously about the influence

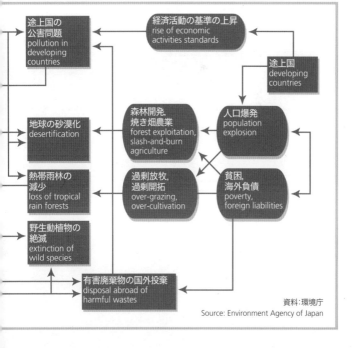

資料:環境庁
Source: Environment Agency of Japan

ります。

Q 日本の援助は環境問題にどのように役だっていますか。

　日本政府は1992年6月に閣議決定された「政府開発援助大綱」において、基本理念として地球環境の保全を掲げるとともに、その原則の中で環境と開発を両立させるとするなど環境重視の姿勢を明確にしています。また、同年リオデジャネイロで開催された地球サミットにおいて、1992年度から5年間で環境ODAを9000億円から1兆円をめどに大幅に拡充・強化することを宣言し、結果的には目標額を大幅に上回る約1兆4400億円を達成しました。

　日本の環境ODAの対象分野は、公害対策(大気汚染防止、水質汚濁防止)や自然環境保全から、森林保全・植林や防災(洪水防御)、居住環境改善(上下水道、廃棄物処理)まで幅広い分野に及んでいます。

　1997年6月の国連環境開発特別総会において、橋本総理大臣より、これらの分野における包括的な協力を進めるために「21世紀

which the growth of international trade may have on the environment.

Q How do Japan's overseas assistance programs contribute to dealing with environmental problems?

The Official Development Assistance Charter, which the Japanese government approved by cabinet resolution in June 1992, puts forward protection of the global environment as a fundamental concept underlying Japan's official development assistance (ODA). It clearly places great importance on environmental issues, and emphasizes the principle that efforts should be directed toward both environmental protection and economic development, and that both types of efforts can be simultaneously successful. At the Rio de Janeiro Earth Summit, which was held in the same year the ODA Charter was approved, the Japanese government announced that it would greatly expand and strengthen environmental ODA, with an assistance goal of between 900 billion and 1 trillion yen during the 5-year period beginning in fiscal 1992. Japanese ODA expenditures on environmental issues during that period in fact surpassed this goal by a large margin, amounting to approximately 1.44 trillion yen.

Japan's environmental ODA is directed to many different fields including pollution countermeasures (prevention of air and water pollution); afforestation and conservation of forests and other aspects of the natural environment; flood-prevention measures; and improving residential environments by improving waste disposal, water supply, and sewerage systems.

At the Special Session of the UN General Assembly on Environment and Development, held in June 1997, Prime Minister Hashimoto announced the "Initiatives for Sustainable

に向けた環境開発支援構想(略称ISD)」を発表しています。今後の環境協力はこの方針の下で行われることになります。

また97年12月に京都において開催された気候変動に関する国際連合枠組み条約第3回締約国会議においては、途上国の温暖化分野の「人づくり」への協力や緩やかな条約で行う円借款「京都イニシアティブ」を発表しています。

また、実際に援助を行う際には、開発に伴う周囲の環境への影響をいかに軽減するかという環境配慮が重要です。このため、国際協力事業団(JICA)、海外経済協力基金(OECF)といった援助実施機関は、環境配慮のためのガイドラインを整備しています。たとえばOECFでは、大規模プロジェクトについての環境アセスメント報告書提出の義務付けや、移転住民への配慮、希少野生動物の保全措置等を講じるよう求めることとしています。

さらに、今後のODA供与に際しては、(1)開発途上国との政策対話、(2)他の先進国・国際機関との協調、(3)NGOとの連携、および(4)環境分野の「人づくり」に対する協力を進めていくのが日本政府の方針です。

Development toward the 21st Century (ISD)" as part of the efforts to promote comprehensive cooperation in these fields. Future environmental assistance will be carried out in accordance with these directives.

At the Third Session of the Conference of the Parties to the United Nations Framework Convention on Climate Change held in Kyoto in December 1997, Japan presented the "Kyoto Initiative," which consists of cooperation in human resources development in the developing countries and offering ODA loans under the most concessional conditions in connection with global warming issues.

In the offering of all types of overseas assistance, it is important to pay attention to ways of minimizing any negative impact on the environment that development brings. The Japan International Cooperation Agency (JICA) and the Overseas Economic Cooperation Fund (OECF) have guidelines for environmental considerations. For example, the OECF's guidelines require the submission of environmental assessment reports for large-scale projects, attention to the problems of people who might be displaced from their residences because of development projects, and measures to protect rare wild animals.

The Japanese government's policy for future ODA highlights the following: (1) policy dialogue with developing countries; (2) coordination with assistance provided by other developed countries and international organizations; (3) cooperation with NGOs; and (4) assistance for "human resources development" in connection with environmental issues.

Q 先進国の廃棄物が
途上国に持ち込まれているらしいですが、
どのような対策が
講じられているのですか。

　　　先進国の社会・経済が発達するにつれて
有害廃棄物の発生量や種類が著しく増大し、
処理が大規模化・複雑化してきています。
このため、より処分しやすい場所を求めて
有害廃棄物がより遠方に輸送されるケース
が増えたのです。

　　　これに対し、1980年代の半ば頃から
OECDやEC(当時)が有害廃棄物の越境移動
に関する規制の必要性を主張し始めるように
なりました。その結果1989年スイスのバー
ゼルで「有害廃棄物の越境移動及びその処
分の規制に関するバーゼル条約」が採択され
(1992年発効)、有害廃棄物の越境移動は条
約の規定に従うこととなりました。

Q 環境と開発を両立させようという
持続可能な開発は
可能なのでしょうか。

　　　「持続可能な開発」とは国連の持続可能な開
発委員会の定義によれば「将来の世代のニ
ーズを満たす能力を損なうことなく現在の世
代のニーズを満たすこと」であるが、この理
念は、ともすれば相反する概念ととらえられ

Q It seems that wastes from the advanced countries are often transported to developing countries for disposal. What sorts of measures are being put in place to deal with this?

With the ongoing development of the societies and economies of the so-called advanced countries, the quantities and types of harmful wastes produced in these countries are increasing greatly, and disposing of these wastes is becoming a more complex and large-scale undertaking. There is thus a growing need for sites where these wastes can be more easily disposed of, and this has involved shipping harmful wastes farther and farther away from their place of origin.

Because of this, from around the middle of the 1980s, the OECD and the then European Community (EC) began emphasizing the need to regulate the transport of hazardous wastes across international borders. As a result, the Basel Convention on the Control of Transboundary Movements of Hazardous Wastes and Their Disposal was adopted in Basel, Switzerland, in 1989. It went into effect in 1992. Thus any transboundary movement of hazardous wastes must be in accordance with the regulations set out in this convention.

Q Is "sustainable development," which aims to simultaneously promote development and environmental protection, possible?

"Sustainable development" means, according to the definition put forth by the UN Commission on Sustainable and Development, "meeting the needs of the present generation without diminishing the capacity to meet the needs of future generations." The most significant element of this concept is

ていた環境と開発を、互いに依存するものとしてとらえたところに、第一の意義があります。

自然保護派対開発促進派、先進国対途上国といった対立の構図を乗り越えて、関係者が手を携えて地球環境の保全に取り組んでいくためには、すべての関係者が「持続可能な開発」というキーワードを念頭に協力していく必要があります。

Q 地球の人口がどんどん増加する中、21世紀の食糧事情はどうなるのですか。人口や食糧問題については、どのような国際協力が行われていますか。

全世界の人口は、今世紀末には62億人、2025年には83億人、2050年には何と98億人に達すると予想されています。人口増加のほとんどは開発途上国で発生していますが、これらの国々では、既に、食糧不足やその他の様々な社会的・経済的な問題が生じています。

この問題に関して、国連の下部機関として国連人口基金が1964年に設置されたほか、1994年9月にはカイロで国際人口開発会議が開催されました。また、NGOとして国際家族計画連盟の下で各国の家族計画団体が活躍しています。

日本政府は94年2月に「人口・エイズに関する地球規模問題イニシアティブ(GII)」を発表し、これに基づいて、94年度から2000年度までの7年間で、ODA総額30億

that it is grounded in the notion of the mutual interdependence of development and environmental protection, two processes which had once been considered mutually exclusive.

In order to deal with the protection of the global environment by overcoming differences between nature protectionists and development promoters, or between developed countries developing countries, we must work together, keeping the key concept of "sustainable development" always firmly in mind.

Q As the Earth's population steadily gets larger, what will the food situation be like in the 21st century? What kinds of international cooperation are being carried out in regard to population and food issues?

The world's population is about 6.2 billion at the end of the 20th century, and is expected to reach 8.3 billion in 2025, and as much as 9.8 billion in 2050. Most of this population increase is taking place in developing countries, where, in many cases, a lack of adequate food is already among the various types of social and economic problems these countries face.

To address these problems, the United Nations Population Fund (UNFPA) was established in 1964, and the UN-sponsored International Conference on Population and Development was held in Cairo in September 1994. Family planning organizations, often affiliated with the International Planned Parenthood Federation (a key NGO), have been active in most countries.

The Japanese government announced its Global Issues Initiative on Population and AIDS (GII) in February 1994, which aims at providing effective assistance to developing countries during the 7-year period between 1994 and 2000.

ドルをめどに開発途上国に対し積極的な協
力を進めています。

食糧問題については、無償資金協力によ
る食料援助や食糧増産援助、農村開発のた
めの技術協力等を通じ、開発途上国に対し
協力しています。

Q 毛皮への反対運動などがありますが、希少動物の保護はどのように行われていますか。

現在、地球上には140万を超える種が確
認されていますが、人間の経済・社会活動
が活発化するに従って急激に種の減少が起
きており、そのペースは、淘汰等によって古
代から続いている自然な種の絶滅のそれを、
大幅に上回っています。

野生生物種の減少が問題なのは、それぞ
れの動物の希少性だけではなく、生物の多様
性そのものが人類の将来に対して無限の可能
性を秘めており、人類の生存を左右する可能
性があるからです。どこにでも居るありふれ
た生物だからといって、決してその存在価値
が劣るということはないのです。

そのような観点から、1992年には地球サ
ミットの場で「生物の多様性に関する条約」
が採択され地球上の生物の多様性の保全と
その構成要素の持続的な利用、および遺伝
資源の利用から生ずる利益の公正かつ衡平
な分配が目指されています。

The total amount of ODA under this program will amount to 3 billion US dollars.

As for food issues, the Japanese government has been cooperating with developing countries in providing grant aid in the form of food, assistance for increasing food production, and technical assistance for the development of farming communities.

Q I've heard about movements against the use of fur products, but in what other ways is the protection of rare animals being promoted?

At present there are known to be over 1.4 million animal and plant species on Earth. But as human beings' economic and other activities intensify, the number of these species is rapidly decreasing. The extent to which they are decreasing is much greater than the pace of natural extinction which has been continuing since ancient times through a process of natural selection.

This decrease in the number of living species is a problem not only because certain animals are rare, but because the very diversity of living species holds untold possibilities relating to our future, including the potential to contribute to mankind's survival. And if some types of plants or animals are commonly found everywhere and seen as "nothing special," the value of their existence is not therefore in any way diminished.

From this perspective, the Convention on Biological Diversity was approved at the 1992 Earth Summit, aiming for the preservation of biological diversity, the sustainable use of animal or plant components, and the fair and equitable sharing of benefits from the utilization of genetic resources.

もっとも、経済的な価値の大きい動植物は、商取引の対象となることにより乱獲されるおそれがより大きいため、1975年には既に条約によりその国際取引が規制されています。(いわゆる「ワシントン条約」とか、正式名称の頭文字をとって「CITES」とか呼ばれる条約です。)

また、野生生物種の減少がもっとも進行しているのはアフリカ、中南米、東南アジアの熱帯地域であり、その背景には急速に進む近代化や人口の増加がありますが、いずれの地域もそのほとんどが開発途上国であり、経済的発展との調和をいかに実現するかが大きな問題となっています。

Q 地球的規模問題に対して日本はアメリカと共同で取り組んでいるようですが、具体的にはどのようなことを行っているのですか。

日本とアメリカは1993年7月に「地球的展望に立った協力のための共通課題(コモン・アジェンダ)」と銘打って、将来の世代が直面することになる重大な地球的規模の課題に取り組み始めました。両国政府と民間が共同して取り組んでおり、世界でもっとも成功している2国間協力の1つです。

コモン・アジェンダはこの5年間に、4つの柱18分野にわたる様々な分野で展開してきました。各プロジェクトは世界的な健康問題、人口の急激な増加、テロリズム、麻薬といった21世紀の課題に対処する方策を模

Needless to say, the fact that certain unusual plants and animals of economic value are the objects of commercial transactions adds to the concern for protecting these species from uncontrolled exploitation. It was to address this problem that such commercial transactions, if on an international scale, have since 1975 been regulated by an international convention, the Convention on International Trade in Endangered Species of Wild Fauna and Flora (CITES).

The decrease in the number of living species is seen most markedly in tropical areas of Africa, Latin America, and Southeast Asia. It is occasioned by rapidly advancing modernization and population growth in these areas, which are made up principally of developing countries. Again at issue is how to harmonize conservation of the natural environment with economic development.

Q I hear that Japan and the United States are working together to tackle problems on a global scale. More specifically, what is being done?

In July 1993, the U.S. and Japan launched the "Common Agenda for Cooperation from a Global Perspective," and set their course to address together serious global issues that future generations will face. The Common Agenda, in which governments, nongovernmental groups and individuals are taking part, has become one of the world's most successful examples of cooperation between two countries.

During its first five years, the Common Agenda has embraced projects in 4 areas, in which 18 initiatives have been taken. Under these projects, which have already produced some encouraging results, the U.S. and Japan are exploring policies for dealing with issues of the 21st century,

索し、成果を挙げてきました。

コモン・アジェンダは、日米関係の幅を広げ、強化し、両国の卓越した2国間協力の基盤の一画を成しており、今後も第3国、国際機関、民間団体および関心を有する一般の方々の参加も得つつ、さらなる発展を目指します。

Q アジア地域でもエイズが広がっているようですが、これまでエイズ問題に対して、国際的にはどのように取り組みがなされ、それに日本はどのように関わって来ていますか。

世界のエイズ患者およびHIV(ヒト免疫不全ウイルス)感染者は1996年12月現在で2260万人に上り、96年だけでも、アフリカ・アジアの開発途上国を中心に310万人が新たに感染したと見られています(UNAIDS推計)。

エイズに対する国際的取り組みは従来、国際機関が個別にエイズ対策を推進するというものでした。しかし、エイズ問題が深刻化する中で、それらの活動の重複・非効率化を避ける目的で、94年に開催された国連経済社会理事会において6つの国連機関(UNICEF、UNDP、UNFPA、UNESCO、WHO、IBRD)が共同スポンサーとして参画するUNAIDS(国連エイズ合同計画)の設置が承認され、96年より正式に発足しました。

such as global health problems, the rapid growth of the world's population, terrorism, and narcotic drugs.

The Common Agenda acts to strengthen U.S.–Japan relations, to broaden their range, and to form an important part of the groundwork for the outstanding cooperative activities being undertaken by the governments and people of the two countries. The Common Agenda aims to further expand its activities through further participation by third countries, international bodies, nongovernmental groups, and interested individuals.

Q I hear AIDS is spreading in Asia, but what is being done internationally to deal with the AIDS problem, and how is Japan involved?

As of December 1996, according to UNAIDS estimates, there were 22.6 million persons infected with the human immunodeficiency virus (HIV), including sufferers from AIDS. During the year 1996 alone, about 3.1 million people were infected, mainly in developing countries of Africa and Asia.

International efforts to address the problem of AIDS had at one time been undertaken separately by international organs. Then, as the AIDS problem grew increasingly acute, in order to avoid inefficiency and an overlapping of AIDS-related programs, a 1994 session of the United Nations Economic and Social Council approved the establishment of the Joint United Nations Program on HIV/AIDS (UNAIDS), which is cosponsored by six UN organs, namely UNICEF, UNDP, the United Nations Population Fund (UNFPA), UNESCO, WHO, and the International Bank for Reconstruction and Development (IBRD, or "World Bank").

UNAIDSの主な任務は(1)関係6機関のエイズ対策事業の調整、(2)エイズに関する研究調査、(3)各国のエイズ対策への助言・技術支援、(4)エイズ問題の広報活動などとなっており、国際的なエイズ対策事業の中心機関として活動しています。

また、1985年にアトランタで開催され、以後毎年開催されている国際エイズ会議も国際的なエイズ対策を検討する場となっています。この会議には世界各地から医学者、科学者をはじめ、患者、HIV感染者、エイズに取り組む国際機関や民間団体などが参加し、エイズに関する様々な問題を討議してきています。

89年にモントリオールで開催された第5回会合では、感染者の基本的人権をうたう「モントリオール宣言」が採択され、各国政府による基本的人権の尊重がエイズ対策を成功させる前提条件であると述べ、国連やNGOは一体となって世界人権宣言が守られるよう活動することを求めています。ちなみに94年の第10回会議はアジア初の会合として、横浜で開催され、世界中から1万人以上の参加を得て大きな成果を生みました。

このほか、94年12月にはパリにおいてWHOと仏政府の共催で、エイズ対策に関するはじめての政府レベルの会合(エイズ・サミット)が開かれ、エイズ対策にかかわる宣言を

This new UNAIDS organization was formally inaugurated in 1996.

The principal tasks of UNAIDS, which is now active as the central intergovernmental organ for AIDS countermeasures, are (1) coordinating the AIDS countermeasures of its six constituent bodies; (2) carrying out AIDS-related surveys and research; (3) providing advice and technical assistance for various countries' AIDS countermeasures; and (4) carrying out public information activities in regard to AIDS issues.

Another forum for the international discussion of AIDS countermeasures is the International AIDS Conference held every year, the first being held in Atlanta in 1985. The participants in these conferences, who come from all parts of the world, include medical doctors and scientists, AIDS patients and others infected with HIV, and representatives of international bodies and nongovernmental groups dealing with AIDS issues, all joining together to discuss the many different aspects of the problem.

The 5th International AIDS Conference, held in Montreal in 1989, adopted the Montreal Declaration emphasizing the fundamental human rights of persons infected with the human immunodeficiency virus. This declaration states that respect for fundamental human rights by every country's government is a prerequisite for the success of AIDS countermeasures, and it calls for joint activities by the United Nations and NGOs to encourage observance of the provisions set forth in the Universal Declaration on Human Rights. The 10th International AIDS Conference, held in Yokohama in 1994, was the first to be held in Asia and produced some impressive results through the participation of over ten thousand people from around the world.

In December 1994, the first government-level conference — known as the "AIDS Summit" — was held in Paris through the joint sponsorship of the World Health Organization (WHO) and the French government. This

採択し、その中で地球規模でエイズ対策を推進する旨の政治的コミットメントを表明しています。日本はこのエイズ・サミットにおいて、人口問題も含めエイズ問題に対する我が国の取り組みとして、2000年までの7年間で人口・エイズ分野においてODA総額30億ドルを目標に開発途上国援助を行う「地球規模問題イニシアティブ」(GII)を発表し、96年度までに約10億ドルの援助を実施しています。

　日本はUNAIDS、WHOに対しても人的、財政的援助を行っているほか、開発途上国で活動するNGOに対しても積極的な支援を行っています。

Q 日本政府とは別に、日本の非政府組織(NGO)はエイズ問題にどう取り組んでいるのですか。

　1995年現在、NGOインフォーメーションネットワークに登録されている日本のエイズ関連の民間団体は56団体に上ります。日本のエイズNGOの多くは活動実績が5年未満となっていますが、それぞれ多様な活動を展開しています。活動内容を大別すると(1)一般社会への啓発、教育活動、(2)活動地域における電話相談サービスの提供、(3)感染者/患者への直接的支援となっています。

　こうしたNGOの活動は、主に国内的なものとなっていますが、94年の横浜国際エイズ会議では多くの日本NGOの参加があり(100用意されたNGO展示ブースのうち30ブースが日本のNGOにより利用)、諸外国のNGOとの間で積極的な国際交流が行われ

meeting adopted a declaration on AIDS countermeasures, voicing a political commitment to promote such programs on a global scale. At this AIDS Summit, Japan announced its Global Issues Initiative (GII), which aims to provide a total of 3 billion US dollars to developing countries during the 7-year period through the year 2000 to assist in dealing with AIDS and population problems. One billion dollars in assistance was given through fiscal 1996.

Additionally, Japan provides financial and personnel assistance to UNAIDS and WHO and gives active financial support for the activities of many NGOs in developing countries.

Q Apart from the Japanese government, in what ways are Japanese NGOs addressing the AIDS problem?

Already in 1995 there were 56 Japan-based, AIDS-related NGOs registered with the NGO Information Network. These NGOs carry out many different types of AIDS-related activities, in most cases begun only in the last five years or so. These types of activities may be roughly classified as follows: (1) activities to educate and inform society as a whole; (2) the provision of telephone consultation services in regions where these groups are active; and (3) direct help to AIDS sufferers and others infected with HIV.

These NGO activities are carried out for the most part within Japan, but many Japan-based NGOs participated in the 1994 International AIDS Conference in Yokohama (where 30 of 100 booths for NGO displays were set up by Japan-based NGOs), and since the conference there has been an active interchange between local NGOs and those based

たほか、アジア諸国のNGOとの協力を推進するアジア太平洋ネットワーク(APCASO)を通じた国際協力も図られています。

従来、日本のエイズ関連のNGOが抱える問題はヒトとカネの不足でした。これは「エイズは日本の問題ではない」といった認識が日本国内に強く、助成や寄付を受けにくい環境にあったこと、また、「エイズは他人事」「性感染は自業自得」といった否定的態度が見られたことに起因しています。

しかし、現在ではエイズ問題に対する理解が進んだこともあり、国や地方自治体で、エイズ対策予算が増え、エイズ対策事業において行政とNGOの連携がみられるようになってきており、NGO指導者養成講座の設置、エイズ研究へのNGOの参加、国際会議へのNGO参加支援等が積極的に行われています。

Q 麻薬問題にはどのような 国際的取り組みがなされてきていますか。

ヘロイン、コカイン、その他の覚醒剤の乱用と不正取引が中核となる「薬物問題」は、今や国境を越えた地球規模の問題としてますます深刻化しつつあります。国連では国連麻薬統制計画(UNDCP)を中心に積極的に対応しています。1990年に国連麻薬特別総会が開催され、「世界行動計画」が採択されるほか、93年には国連総会で麻薬についての特別会合が開催され、各国が麻薬撲滅強化にプライオリティを置くことを再確認し、

abroad. International cooperation with NGOs in other Asian countries is being carried out through the APCASO network (Asia/Pacific Council of AIDS Service Organizations).

In the past, Japan's AIDS-related NGOs have faced problems of insufficient money and personnel. Within Japan there was a prevailing idea that "AIDS is not a problem for Japan," which made it difficult to get either government assistance or private contributions. This was related not just to the notion that "AIDS is the problem of other people" but also to the notion that "infection through sexual activity is a deserved consequence of one's own doing."

However, understanding of the AIDS problem has now progressed, national and local government budgets for dealing with AIDS have increased, and we see cooperation between the government and NGOs in carrying out AIDS countermeasures. Programs are being actively promoted to establish training courses for AIDS-related NGO guidance personnel, to help NGOs take part in AIDS-related research, and to help NGOs participate in international conferences.

Q In what ways is the problem of narcotic drugs being addressed internationally?

The so-called "drug problem," centered around the proliferation and illegal sale of heroin, cocaine and other harmful stimulant drugs, is one of global scope, going beyond national borders, and it is becoming more and more acute. The United Nations is actively addressing this problem through the United Nations International Drug Control Program (UNDCP). In 1990, the Special Session of the UN General Assembly on Narcotic Drugs was held and adopted the Global Program of Action. In 1993, the special meeting of the UN General Assembly was held to address the drug

「世界行動計画」履行強化を目指した決議を
採択しています。また、98年には、国連総
会麻薬特別会期が開催されました。

　サミットにおいても85年のボン・サミッ
トで議題として取り上げられて以来、議長声
明で国際協力の強化が強調され種々の対応
がなされています。また、先進各国の薬物関
連の協力のための情報交換、協議の場とし
てダブリン・グループが90年に日、米、EC
諸国などにより発足されています。条約面で
の整備も従来から進められており、61年に
麻薬単一条約、71年に向精神薬条約、88年
に麻薬新条約が採択され、各国とも早期批
准を進めています。

　こうした動きに対し、日本は上記の3条約
をいち早く批准するとともに、UNDCPへの
財政支援を中心とした貢献を行っており、国
連麻薬委員会等の薬物統制関連の各種国際
会議、フォーラムの場においても積極的に情
報交換を行い、麻薬問題に対する国際協力
を進めています。

issue, where it was reaffirmed that each country should give priority to strengthening drug eradication efforts, and a resolution was adopted to carry out the Global Program of Action with greater vigor. A UN General Assembly Special Session to address the drug issue was held in 1998.

Since the drug problem was first taken up at the Bonn G-7 Summit in 1985, declarations by the conveners of the G-7 summits have emphasized international cooperation in tackling the problem and have given impetus to various policy measures. An important forum for discussion and for the exchange of information on the joint efforts of advanced countries to mitigate the drug problem is the Dublin Group, which got under way in 1990, with representatives from Japan, the United States, and the EC. Progress has been made in establishing international treaties that address the drug issue. The Single Convention on Narcotic Drugs had been adopted by the United Nations in 1961, followed by the Convention on Psychotropic Substances in 1971, and the United Nations Convention against Illicit Traffic in Narcotic Drugs and Psychotropic Substances in 1988. It is hoped these will be ratified by all national governments.

In response to such developments, the Japanese government was quick to ratify the three UN conventions and has contributed financially to the work of the UN International Drug Control Program. Japan actively engages in the exchange of information with various international conferences and forums, including the UN Commission on Narcotic Drugs, for the control of narcotic drugs, and encourages international cooperation in dealing with the problems involved.

人物紹介

エイズと
性の
差別と戦う

池上さんの事務所でまず目につくのは、CONDOMING BOOK、SAFER SEX GUIDE BOOK といったタイトルのパンフレットです。前者は特に若い女性たちに、そして後者はゲイの人たちに、現在も世界で広がりつつある HIV 感染（AIDS）から身を守るために、セックスの時にはコンドームを使用することを呼びかけています。

「ぷれいす
（PLACE）東京」
主宰者
いけがみ ちずこ
池上千寿子
Ikegami
Chizuko
**Facilitator
of PLACE
TOKYO**

池上さんは、1969年に大学を出て、しばらく出版社に勤めていましたが、やがてフリーの記者となり、その後、日系1世の人たちの歴史を掘り起こそうと、サンフランシスコに渡りました。その取材の中で、今も続く日系人たちの苦難の生活の歴史を知るうちに、彼女は、日系人の生活向上のためのNGOの活動に加わることになっていきました。

しかし、日系1世たちの問題以外に、池上さんがもう1つ興味を向け続けていたのは、人間の「心と体と性」の問題でした。

1982年、彼女は「性と社会のための太平洋センター」を主宰しているハワイ大学のミルトン・ダイヤモンド教授を訪れて、研究生にしてほしいと頼み込みました。池上さんの熱心さと意気込みに応えて、教授は池上さんを快く受け入れてくれました。そして、このハワイで池上さんはエイズの問題と関わることになるのです。

Fighting Discrimination Related to Sex and AIDS

The first thing you find in Ms. Ikegami's office is her pamphlets entitled *Condoming Book* and *Safer Sex Guide Book*. The first is especially designed for young women and the second for so-called "gay" people, but both appeal for the use of condoms when having sex, to guard against infection with the human immunodeficiency virus (HIV) that is now spreading throughout the world and that is the cause of the acquired immunodeficiency syndrome (AIDS).

Ms. Ikegami graduated from college in 1969 and worked for some time in a publishing firm. Later, after becoming a free-lance journalist, she went to San Francisco to explore the history of first-generation immigrants from Japan. In the process of information-gathering, she became familiar with the history of the still-difficult lives of Japanese immigrants and joined in the activities of an NGO established to help them improve their lives.

However, in addition to the problems of the Japanese immigrants, Ms. Ikegami came to have a sustained interest in still another set of issues, namely, those concerned with people's "hearts, bodies, and sex."

In 1982, she visited Prof. Milton Diamond, who led the Pacific Center for Sex and Society at the University of Hawaii and asked if she could become one of his research students. Responding to Ms. Ikegami's enthusiasm and eagerness to work with him, Prof. Diamond gladly agreed to take her into his group. In this way, Ms. Ikegami became involved, in Hawaii, with issues related to AIDS.

人物
紹介

　エイズという新しく発見された性感染症(STD=Sexually Transmitted Disease)が最初に報告されたのは1981年のことです。彼女の友人の知人である女性が輸血の血液からHIVに感染するなど、彼女の周辺で、1年の間に3人が亡くなりました。そのエイズ感染者たちが、ただエイズであるというだけで差別される現実に、池上さんは強い憤りをおぼえるようになっていきました。

　池上さんは、最初は2年で日本に帰るつもりでしたが、1988年までハワイ大学で勉強を続け、その後、ハワイのエイズのNGOに参加して、エイズ患者に対する支援活動を始めました。

　1991年に帰国した池上さんは、翌年、東京都のエイズ専門家の会議の委員になるなど、さまざまなエイズ問題の研究や啓蒙活動に関わるようになりました。そして、自らの活動の拠点として「ぷれいす東京」を作ったのです。

　エイズの予防のためにはコンドームを使った正しい性行為をすること、HIVに感染していることがわかっていても、コンドームを正しく使えばセックスを楽しむことができること、そして、エイズに対して差別意識を持つのは間違いなのだということを、池上さんは呼びかけています。同時に、エイズ感染者に対するケア活動も繰り広げるなど、今日も無償の活動を続けているのです。

Asian AIDS Conference (1995).
Conference Chairperson
Ikegami Chizuko is third
from the right

The newly discovered STD (sexually transmitted disease) known as AIDS had first been reported in 1981. Yet in the space of a year, three acquaintances of Ms. Ikegami's died of AIDS, including a female friend who had had been infected with HIV through a blood transfusion. Ms. Ikegami came to feel angry over the fact that persons infected with HIV were discriminated against merely as a result of this misfortune.

Although she had at first planned to return to Japan after two years in Hawaii, Ms. Ikegami continued to study at the University of Hawaii until 1988, and then joined an AIDS-related NGO in Hawaii, and began taking part in its activities to help AIDS sufferers.

She returned to Japan in 1991 and the following year became involved in various types of research and public education activities dealing with AIDS issues, serving, for example, as a member of a conference of AIDS specialists in Tokyo. Then she established PLACE (Positive Living And Community Empowerment) TOKYO as headquarters for her own activities.

Ms. Ikegami is calling for safer sexual activities using condoms to prevent the spread of AIDS. She argues that it is a mistake to discriminate against persons living with HIV or suffering from AIDS. She says, for example, that any person, regardless of HIV status, can enjoy safer sex if he/she uses a condom properly. She is continuing her volunteer work today, expanding her activities to include care for people living with HIV/AIDS.

世界文化・教育の
保護・発展のために

Protecting and
Developing Culture
and Education

Chapter

Q 日本はカンボジアの
国民的な文化遺産である
アンコール遺跡の保存に
協力していますが、
実際、どのような活動をしていますか。

　　　世界各地に存在する文化遺跡や文化財は、
人類共通の貴重な財産であるにもかかわら
ず、十分な保存・修復が行われないまま消滅
の危機に瀕しているものも少なくありませ
ん。その代表的な例がカンボジアのアンコー
ル遺跡群です。

　　　アンコール遺跡群は、アンコール王朝(9
〜13世紀)が作ったクメール文化の中心的存
在です。しかし、長年にわたる内戦などの影

Investigation work at Prasat Suor Prat, ▲
Angkor Thom, Cambodia (Photo: N. Matsukura)

Q What sorts of activities is Japan engaged in to help with the preservation of the Angkor Monuments, Cambodia's national cultural heritage?

There are many cultural sites and cultural properties that are the valuable and shared heritage of all humankind which are on the verge of disappearing unless sufficient attention is given to their conservation and restoration. An important example is the Angkor architectural monuments in Cambodia.

The Angkor remains are a symbol of the traditional Khmer culture of Cambodia created during the Angkor Dynasty (9th to 13th centuries). However, due to long years

響により損傷の状態が激しく、カンボジア国内の情勢は落ち着きを見せてきたとはいえ、その保存のためには、財政的にも、技術的にも、多くの問題を抱えていました。

そこで日本政府は1998年に、アンコール遺跡救済チーム(JSA; Japanese Government Team for Safeguarding Angkor)を結成し、ユネスコの中に設置した文化遺産保存日本信託基金を通じ、修復、保存のための協力をすることとしました。JSAは、これまでに16回にわたり調査団を派遣し、段階的な修復が進められています。

単なる修復作業だけではなく、今後の遺跡修復のための技術をカンボジアの人々に身につけてもらうため、修復現場で現地の学生を対象に研修を行ったり、修復作業を行うカンボジア人スタッフに対しても、それぞれの適性に合った技術習得のための訓練を施すのも目的です。

アンコール遺跡群の保存修復のためには、1993年以降、日本とフランスが共同議長となって、年3～4回、プノンペンおよびシエムリアップで国際会議が開催され、関係国や機関の間での協調が図られています。日本国内でもJSAのほか、日本国内の研究機関、NGOやボランティア等の関係者も参加して、日本は、いわばAll Japanの体制で遺跡の修復に協力をしていると言えます。

of civil war, they have been severely damaged and, even though the internal situation seems to be stabilized, Cambodia faces many financial and technological problems regarding their preservation.

In 1998, the Japanese government organized the Japanese Government Team for Safeguarding Angkor (JSA), which has been implementing the preservation project of the Angkor remains through the Japanese Trust Fund for the Preservation of the World Cultural Heritage established within the framework of UNESCO. The JSA has dispatched 16 survey missions and it is carrying out step-by-step preservation work.

The JSA activities go beyond mere preservation work to include training for local students at the restoration site, so as to familiarize Cambodians with techniques of restoration in the future. Appropriate training is also being provided to help Cambodian project staff members acquire skills for supervising restoration activities.

In order to help with the preservation of the Angkor monuments, an international coordinating committee, since 1993 jointly chaired by Japan and France holds three or four meetings a year both in Phnom Penh and Siem Reap and in this way various efforts are coordinated among the countries and organizations concerned. Japan cooperates in the Angkor preservation work in what one might call an "All-Japan" fashion, with the participation, in addition to the JSA, of various relevant Japanese research bodies, NGOs, and volunteers.

Q 世界文化遺産とは何ですか。
これら世界文化遺産を始めとする
世界の文化財の保護のためには
日本はどのようなことを行っていますか。

　世界文化遺産とは、世界153ヵ国が加盟
している「世界の文化遺産および自然遺産
の保護に関する条約（Convention Con-
cerning the Protection of the World
Cultural and Natural Heritage）」に基づ
き世界遺産リストに記載された、万里の長城
やピラミッドなどをはじめとする普遍的価値
を持つ文化遺産を指します。

　現在、世界各国の418件（1997年12月
現在）の建造物等が記載されており、日本
国内では、「法隆寺地域の仏教建造物」、「姫
路城」、「古都京都の文化財」、「白川郷・五
箇山の合掌造り集落」、「原爆ドーム」、「厳島
神社」の6ヵ所が記載されています。

　これらの遺産の保護のために、日本を始
め条約を締結した国の拠出により「世界遺
産基金」が設けられており、この基金で各
遺産の保護のための調査、研究、専門家派
遣、研修、機材供与、資金協力などが行わ
れ、国際社会全体による各遺産の保護・保
存が図られています。

　日本政府は、このような世界遺産基金を
通じての文化遺産保護協力に先立ち、文化
遺産の保存修復のため、1989年に「文化遺
産保存日本信託基金」をユネスコに創設し、
現在までに合計2615万ドルの拠出を行って

Q What exactly are "World Cultural Heritage Sites"? And what sorts of things is Japan doing to protect these World Cultural Heritage Sites and other cultural properties in the world?

The term "World Cultural Heritage Sites" refers to cultural properties of outstanding universal value (including, for example, the Great Wall of China and the Pyramids of Egypt) which have been registered on the World Heritage List in accordance with the Convention Concerning the Protection of the World Cultural and Natural Heritage, subscribed to by 153 nations.

As of December 1997, 418 architectural and other heritages throughout the world were so registered. Six of these sites are in Japan: the Buddhist Monuments in the Hōryūji Temple Area, Himeji Castle, the Historic Monuments of Ancient Kyoto, the Historic Villages of Shirakawa-gō and Gokayama, the Hiroshima Peace Memorial (Genbaku Dome), and the Itsukushima Shrine.

To protect these heritages the World Heritage Fund has been established with monetary contributions from Japan and other member nations of the above-mentioned Convention. Through this fund, efforts are being made by international society as a whole for the protection and preservation of these heritages in the form of studies, research, the dispatch of experts, on-the-job training, the provision of equipment and materials, and financial cooperation.

Already before the start of its cultural heritage preservation work through the World Heritage Fund, the Japanese government established the Japanese Trust Fund for the Preservation of the World Cultural Heritage within UNESCO in 1989. As of 1998, total expenditures were US

います。この基金は、崩壊の危機に瀕している世界の文化遺跡の保護に用いられており、日本から専門家を派遣して、修復作業を行ったり、また、そのための事前調査や現地のスタッフの研修に協力したりしています。我が国はこの基金を通じ、これまでに、カンボジアのアンコール遺跡群やパキスタンのモヘンジョダロ遺跡など、18の遺跡保存事業に協力しています。

また、主にアジアの舞踊・音楽等の伝統芸能、陶芸・染織等の伝統工芸などの無形文化財の保存と振興を図るため、1993年より、日本政府はユネスコに「無形文化財保存振興日本信託基金」を創設しました。この基金に対し、日本は、毎年拠出を行い、緊急性が高いと判断される文化財から順次に保存する事業に協力しています。

Q 開発途上国が抱える、文化の振興や教育文化水準の向上という問題に対し、日本はどのようなことをしていますか。

開発途上国では、社会の経済的発展とともに、その国の固有の文化の維持・振興に対する関心が高まり、文化面を含む視野からバランスのとれた国家開発のための努力がなされています。こうした努力に対し、日本政府は、伝統文化や文化遺産の保存、芸術・教育活動への支援を行っており、「文化無償協力」はその重要な柱の1つになってい

$26.15 million. This fund has been used for the preservation of world cultural heritage sites that are in imminent danger of disintegration. The work supported by the fund includes the dispatch of experts who take part in preservation and restoration efforts. Cooperation also includes preliminary surveys and the training of local project staff. This fund has so far provided assistance to preservation work at 18 sites, including the Angkor Monuments in Cambodia and the Mohenjo-Daro archaeological site in Pakistan.

In 1993, the Japanese government established the Japanese Trust Fund for the Preservation and Promotion of Intangible Cultural Properties, within the framework of UNESCO, in order to preserve and promote, mainly in Asia, such cultural forms as traditional performing arts (dance, music, etc.) and traditional arts and crafts such as ceramics and the dyeing of fabrics. Japan makes contributions to this fund each year, cooperating on a prioritized basis in the preservation of those cultural assets that are judged to be most urgently in need of support.

Q What is Japan doing to contribute to the resolution of developing countries' problems in promoting culture and improving educational and cultural levels?

In the developing countries, there is rising interest not only in the economic development of their societies, but also in the maintenance and promotion of each country's indigenous culture, and efforts are being made to achieve national development from a balanced point of view that includes the cultural sphere. The Japanese government supports such efforts by helping with the preservation of cultural heritages and traditional culture, as well as assisting artistic and edu-

ます。

日本の文化無償協力は、文化財・文化遺産の保存活用、文化関係の公演・展示の開催、教育・研究振興などに必要とされる機材の購入のための資金を贈与するものです。

相手国の要請に基づいて審査を行い、劇場など文化施設への音響機材、スポーツ機材、大学・研究所など教育施設への視聴覚機材などが供与されています。1997年までに、114の開発途上国に、延べ908件、総額では373億円の供与を行っています。

さらに、照明や音響技術から教育、あるいは各種スポーツといった人材育成のための文化諸分野での指導、助言を行うための専門家の派遣、招聘を行っています。

また、開発途上国の国造りには、教育水準の向上が欠かせません。そのために青年海外協力隊では、1968年に中学校の理数科の先生をタンザニアに派遣して以来、これまでに、38ヵ国に延べ1200人を超える隊員を、小・中・高校教師として派遣して来ています。

Q 日本とアジアの若者たちの交流を、日本政府はどのような形で支援していますか。

まず、アジア・ユース・フェローシップ・

cational activities. Among these, Cultural Grant Aid of Japan is an important element.

Cultural Grant Aid of Japan refers to funding for the preservation of cultural properties and heritages, the holding of cultural performances and exhibitions, and the purchase of equipment and materials needed for promoting educational and research activities.

The Japanese government examines each project based on the requests from recipient countries and provides, for example, sound equipment for theaters and other cultural facilities, sports equipment, or audiovisual equipment for universities, research institutes and other educational facilities. Until 1997, a total of 908 such grants were made to 114 developing countries, amounting to 39.3 billion yen.

In addition, specialists have been sent abroad and invitations have been extended for coming to Japan for consultation and guidance to assist human resources development in such culture-related fields as lighting, acoustic technology, education, and sports.

The improvement of educational levels is an indispensable factor in successful nation-building in the developing countries. To assist with these efforts, over 1,200 members of the Japan Overseas Cooperation Volunteers have over the years — beginning with the sending of science and mathematics teachers to middle schools in Tanzania in 1968 — served as teachers in elementary, middle, and higher schools in 38 countries.

Q In what ways is the Japanese government supporting exchanges between Japanese and other Asian young people?

First of all, there is the Asia Youth Fellowship Program

プログラムがあります。これは、アジア諸国の人材育成と日本の青少年の間との交流を図るもので、アジア諸国の若者を対象に、マレーシアで約1年間にわたり日本語を始めとする勉強をしてもらい、その後文部省の国費留学生として日本で修士・博士号を修得するための機会を与える制度です。

そのほか、アジア諸国の高校生を日本に招待するとともに、また我が国の高校生をアジア諸国に派遣し、1年間にわたり一般家庭にホームステイさせて高校に留学させるコースもあります。

また、日本政府では、中国、韓国、東南アジアなどアジア諸国から毎年、次世代を担う1000人近い若者たちを日本に招待しています。日本の実情を見てもらったり、日本の若者たちとの交流の機会を持ったり、各界の人々との交流等を通じて、これらアジア諸国の若い世代の正確な対日理解の推進を図るためです。

これらアジア諸国との青年交流事業の中で、ユニークな事業としては、「東南アジア青年の船」があります。これは、18歳から30歳の日本と東南アジア各国の若者たちが同じ船に乗って、約50日ほどかけて東南アジア各国を回り、生活を共にし、交流活動を行うものです。日本と東南アジア諸国の青年たち相互の友好と理解を促進する目的で、20年以上続けられています。

毎年、航海を終えて下船する時には、船の上で交流を温めた各国からの仲間たちが、涙を流しながら別れを惜しむ光景が見られるなど、この事業は各国からの参加する青年た

which aims at developing human resources in Asian countries and giving opportunities for exchange among Asian and Japanese young people. It provides opportunities for young people from Asian countries to study the Japanese language and other subjects for a year in Malaysia, after which they are given opportunities to obtain master's or doctoral degrees in Japan supported by Japanese Ministry of Education (Mombushō) scholarships.

Among other things, the Japanese government also invites high school students from other Asian countries to Japan and sponsors Japanese high school students who go to Asian countries to spend a year in high schools while staying with ordinary families.

Furthermore, the Japanese government invites about 1,000 promising young people from China, Korea and Southeast Asian countries to Japan each year. The purpose of this program is to give them opportunities to experience the real life of Japan and to have contacts with Japanese young people and others in various walks of life, and in this way to foster an accurate understanding of Japan among the younger generation in these Asian countries.

A unique enterprise among these youth exchange activities with Asian countries is the Ship for Southeast Asian Youth. Japanese and Southeast Asian young people from the ages of 18 to 30 board a ship together and travel to several Southeast Asian countries for about 50 days, living together and enjoying various activities. This program started more than 20 years ago, with the aim of promoting mutual friendship and understanding among young people from Japan and Southeast Asia.

Each year, at the end of the voyage the participants can be seen bidding farewell with tears in their eyes, and it may truly be said that this program creates unforgettable, lifelong memories for the young participants.

ちに、生涯忘れ得ぬ思い出を作ると言われています。

このほか、我が国へ留学した経験を元に母国で活躍している元日本留学生を再度日本に招く、20年近く続いている招待事業があります。これは、元留学生相互の親睦を深め、日本について再認識する機会を提供することを目的としたものです。このプログラムで訪日した元留学生たちには、改めて日本国内の教育・研究機関や産業施設の視察・見学をしてもらい、留学時から変化した日本の姿を認識してもらっています。

Q 日本人と諸外国の人々が相互理解を深めていくため、どのようなことが行われていますか。

日本政府は1983年から84年にかけて「留学生10万人計画」を提唱して以来、諸外国からの留学生の受け入れを積極的に推進して来ました。現在5万人を超える外国人留学生が日本国内の大学等で研究を行っています。外務省では、各国にある日本大使館や総領事館を通じて留学希望者への情報提供、国費留学生の募集・選考を実施しています。また、文部省の関係団体では、留学に関する情報をインターネットで世界各国に向け発信もしています。また、留学生の帰国後も日本に関心を持ち続けてもらうために、留学生OB会の組織造りの支援などをしています。

日本と諸外国の文化交流や、国際相互理解を深め、世界の文化の育成および人類の

In additon, there is a program which invites back to Japan former foreign students who now take an active part in various fields in their home countries. This program has continued for nearly 20 years, deepening mutual friendships among these former students and providing them with opportunities to renew their acquaintance with Japan. This program gives former students opportunities to visit Japanese educational, research, and industrial facilities and to see with their own eyes the ways in which Japan has changed since they were students.

Q What kinds of things are being done to help people in Japan and in other countries deepen mutual understanding?

Since the Japanese government proposed the "100,000 Foreign Students Plan" in 1983–84, it has been actively promoting efforts to welcome students from other countries. At present, over 50,000 foreign students are pursuing studies and research in Japanese universities. Through Japanese embassies and consulates, the Ministry of Foreign Affairs provides information for people interested in studying in Japan and takes applications for Japanese government scholarships. In addition, various organizations affiliated with the Ministry of Education provide information about study in Japan to countries throughout the world using the Internet. They also give assistance for organizing alumni associations of former foreign students to help them keep up contacts with Japan after they return to their home countries.

The Japan Foundation was established in 1972 to deepen cultural exchange and mutual understanding between

福祉に貢献することを目的に国際交流基金が1972年に設立されました。同基金では、日本文化を紹介できる様々な分野の専門家等、多様な分野の人々を海外へ派遣したり、諸外国の同様の人々を日本に招いたりして、それぞれの分野での交流を促進させる人物交流事業を進めています。

国際交流基金アジアセンターは、アジア各国が21世紀に向けて相互理解を深め、共通の問題に協力して取り組むことを願い、各国の多様な文化を尊重しながらアジアと大洋州地域が共有しうる新しい文化・価値観を育むことを目的に設立されたものです。

具体的には、アジアと大洋州地域の大学・研究機関の間での共同研究プロジェクトや知的交流セミナーの支援などを通じて、アジア地域の知的交流を推進したり、アジア各国の美術・工芸品や古文書の修復・保存を行って行く上で必要な環境作りや、音楽、舞踊、工芸技術などの記録や担い手の育成を目的とした事業に協力したりしています。また、アジア諸国の文化を日本国内に紹介する事業を行っています。

アメリカ合衆国を対象とした交流事業として、日本が米国と協調して地球規模の問題に取り組み、世界に貢献していくことや、相互理解に基づいて強固な日米関係を実現するため日米各界各層における対話と交流を推進することを目的に、「日米センター」が1991年に設立されました。

日米センターでは、日米両国の研究機関、

Japan and other countries and also to contribute to the development of culture throughout the world and to the welfare of humankind. This government-financed foundation promotes people-to-people exchanges in various fields, dispatching experts and other persons in many fields who make Japanese culture better known abroad, as well as inviting people from other countries to come to Japan for similar purposes.

The Japan Foundation Asia Center was established with the wish that Asian countries might deepen mutual understanding as we approach the 21st century and to cooperate in dealing with common problems. It is hoped that it will contribute to fostering new values and cultural perspectives shared throughout the Asia-Pacific region, while respecting cultural diversity.

The Asia Center's activities include cooperative efforts to promote intellectual exchange through seminars and projects for joint research among universities and research bodies in the Asia-Pacific region; efforts to create the necessary environments for preservation and restoration of the region's arts, crafts, and written materials; the documentation of musical, dance, and craft skills; and the training of persons who inherit such skills. In these ways, the Asia Center helps introduce the cultures of other Asian countries to Japan.

As for exchanges with the United States of America, the Center for Global Partnership was established in 1991 to promote dialogue and exchange at many levels between Japan and the United States with the purpose of achieving sound Japanese-American relations based on mutual understanding. It also seeks to promote collaboration between Japan and the United and States in tackling global issues, thereby contributing to improvements in the world's welfare.

The Center for Global Partnership gives financial assis-

大学等が共同で政策指向型の研究を行う際に、資金面での助成を行っています。また、政界、経済界、メディアなどの有識者が地球規模の問題やその他の先進国共通の課題について議論する会議やセミナーについても支援しています。さらには、地域・草の根レベルでの日米間の相互理解を推進する事業に対しても助成を行っています。

アジア・欧州諸国間の交流では、「アジア・欧州ヤングリーダーズ・シンポジウム(AEYLS)」があります。これは、21世紀の世界を担うアジア・欧州地域のヤング・リーダー的な立場で活躍する人々の交流を通じ、アジア・欧州地域の関係強化と相互理解を推進するためのシンポジウムで、1997年3月に、第1回のアジア・欧州ヤングリーダーズ・シンポジウムが日本で開催されました。「21世紀の新たなアジア・欧州協力の探求」をテーマに開催されたこのシンポジウムでは、アジア・欧州25ヵ国/機関(EU)の若手有識者、学者、ビジネスマン等が日本政府により招待され、経済、情報化など7つのテーマに基づき活発な意見交換が行われました。同様の分野で活躍している各国からの参加者の間に大きなネットワークができ、その後も交流が続いています。なお、第2回目のシンポジウムは、1998年5月にオーストリアで開催され、第3回シンポジウムは1999年に韓国で開催される予定です。

tance for policy-oriented research carried out jointly by universities and research bodies in Japan and United States. It also supports conferences and seminars on global issues and other issues common to developed countries in which intellectuals in the fields of politics, business, and the media participate. It further provides assistance to projects which promote mutual understanding between Japan and the United States at the regional and grassroots levels.

As for exchanges between the countries of Asia and Europe, the Asia-Europe Young Leaders Symposium (AEYLS), which is designed to promote mutual understanding and stronger relations between the Asian and European regions, gives opportunities to exchange views to "young leaders" in Asia and Europe who will play important roles in the world of the 21st century. The first symposium was held in Japan in March 1997.

Young scholars, businessmen, and intellectuals representing 25 Asian and European countries and the European Union (EU) were invited by the Japanese government to take part in this first symposium, which dealt with the general theme of "seeking new cooperation between Asia and Europe in the 21st century." There was a lively discussion on seven topics such as economics and the growth of an information society. A large network has been created among participants who are active in similar fields, and exchanges among them are continuing. The second symposium was held in Austria in May 1998 and the third one is scheduled to be held in Korea in 1999.

Q 日米間で市民レベルで交流したいとき、何らかの公的な支援を受けることが可能ですか。

国際交流基金の日米センターでは、地域レベル・草の根レベルの交流事業に対し助成を行っています。この助成事業には2種類あり、1つは、日米間の相互理解を推進するための事業や、地球規模の問題についての理解の促進を目的とした「教育アウトリーチ」があります。

もう1つは、日米間の様々な層の人々の対話の促進を目的とした交流事業を支援しています。この交流事業には、具体的な問題解決のための地域レベル、コミュニティーレベルでの交流や、日米両国が今日直面する国内問題や国際問題について話し合うものが含まれています。

これまでに、日米姉妹都市の会議、米国ノースカロライナ州の教育関係者が同州の教育問題の改善を図るため日本の教育現場を視察し、帰国後に政策提言を行うプログラム、災害時における社会的弱者のための防災・救援システムを検討するための、奈良県のNGOによる米国での調査活動など、バラエティーに富んだ事業に対する助成が行われています。

なお、助成を受けるためには、日米両国にある国際交流基金日米センターに申請し審査を受けることが必要です。

Q Is there any sort of government support for Japanese-American exchanges at the level of ordinary citizens?

The Center for Global Partnership of the Japan Foundation gives financial support for two categories of cultural exchange programs at the regional and grassroots levels. The first, under the name of "educational outreach," aims at promoting mutual understanding between Japan and the United States and a more widespread understanding of global issues.

Supported programs of the second type are usually more specific and seek to promote communication and dialogue between people of all walks of life in Japan and the United States. These exchange programs include regional and community-level exchanges aimed to help resolve specific problems and also include opportunities for the discussion of domestic and international issues both nations face today.

Assistance has been extended to a wide variety of programs, including meetings of representatives of Japanese and American sister cities, a program through which educators from the state of North Carolina visited schools in Japan as part of their activities of preparing policy recommendations aimed at improvements in the educational field in their home state, and study-visits to the United States by an NGO in Nara Prefecture for the purpose of learning systems for preventing disasters and helping socially disadvantaged persons when disasters occur.

Persons or groups interested in receiving such financial assistance may apply to the offices of the Center for Global Partnership in Japan or the United States and must go through a selection process.

Q
日本文化の紹介や伝統芸能の
海外公演などについて、
日本政府はどのような形で
支援しているのでしょうか。

外務省と国際交流基金は、従来より、歌舞伎や生け花などの日本の伝統文化や現代日本の芸術・文化を、各国にある日本大使館・総領事館や国際交流基金の事務所を通じて紹介しています。

歌舞伎、和太鼓、邦楽、オペラなどの日本の優れた舞台芸術・芸能の公演が海外から望まれていながら、経費の条件が整わないために実行が困難になっている場合、公演団体に対し、経費の一部の助成を行っています。また、原則として途上国を対象に中・大型の公演団の経費を負担して派遣する場合もあります。

生け花、邦楽や現代舞踊などの専門家を短期間海外に派遣して、各国でレクチャー、デモンストレーション等を行ったりもしています。また、空手や柔道を始めとするスポーツの専門家を派遣したりもしています。

The Kudara Kannon on exhibit at the Louvre Museum in Paris

日本の伝統芸術や美術の紹介も積極的に行われています。国際交流基金が保有する日本の伝統的な凧・独楽、版画、伝統陶芸、人形、現代日本のポスターセット等の巡回展が世界各国で行われています。これらの巡回展が各国で開催される際には、通常、現地の新聞・テレビなどで紹介され、多くの人々が会場を訪れ、日本文化の紹介に役立っています。

Q In what ways does the Japanese government support efforts to make Japanese culture, including presentations of traditional performing arts, better known abroad?

The Ministry of Foreign Affairs and the Japan Foundation have been making efforts to introduce to people abroad various aspects of Japan's traditional culture inculding *kabuki* and *ikebana*, as well as aspects of Japan's contemporary art and culture through embassies, consulates, and Japan Foundation offices abroad.

In cases where there is a strong desire abroad for presentations of outstanding examples of Japanese stage art (for example *kabuki*, *wadaiko* drum performances, *hōgaku* musical programs and modern opera), but bringing them to reality is difficult due to financial restraints, assistance may be provided to cover a part of the expenses of the performing groups. Medium-size and large performing groups may be sent with complete government financial support in certain cases, principally when they perform in developing countries.

Specialists in such arts as *ikebana*, *hōgaku*, and modern dance are sent abroad for short periods to give lectures and demonstrations. Specialists in karate, judo and other sports may also be assisted in travels and activities abroad.

Active efforts are being made to introduce other Japanese traditional arts and crafts abroad. The Japan Foundation sponsors touring exhibits of traditional Japanese kites, tops, dolls, woodblock prints and pottery, as well as sets of posters depicting contemporary Japan. These touring exhibits, which are visited by large numbers of people and are discussed in local newspapers and on television, play an important role in introducing Japanese culture to other countries.

　また、今日の日本の美術状況と優れた現代作家を紹介することを目的としたビエンナーレなどの国際展への参加や、商業ベースに乗りにくい展覧会に対し、経費の一部を助成しています。

　単発の文化交流行事のほか、時には、現地の日本大使館、国際交流基金、そして現地の日系企業、日本人会などが協力して、いくつもの文化交流行事を集中的に実施する日本文化フェスティバルなどの大型の日本紹介事業が開催されることもあります。

　諸外国の人々がこれらの日本文化を紹介するデモンストレーションや展覧会を訪れることにより、日本に対し一層の親近感を抱くケースが多く、日本が諸外国との友好親善を進める上でも、今後とも地道な日本文化の紹介を続けていく必要があると言えます。

Q 若い外国人を英語の教師として招き、日本の中高等学校で外国語の助手として、また地方自治体の国際交流員として働いてもらうJETプログラムは10周年を迎えたそうですが、これまでの成果はどんなものでしょうか。

　このJETプログラムを通じ、外国人の指導助手から英語を習うことにより、英会話に対する関心の増大が見られ、生徒の英語に

Financial assistance is also provided to cover a part of the costs of participating in international exhibitions like the Biennale that introduce the Japanese fine arts scene and outstanding contemporary artists. Individual artists may also be assisted in holding overseas exhibitions when this would be difficult on a commercial basis.

In addition to events which are organized on an ad hoc basis, from time to time there are large-scale events to introduce Japan abroad in the form of Japanese Cultural Festivals, and the like, which bring together a number of different cultural exchange activities and are held with the cooperation of local Japanese embassies and the Japan Foundation, as well as local Japan-based business enterprises and local associations of Japanese residents.

Visits by people overseas to such performances and exhibitions of Japanese culture typically bring about positive sentiments and a greater sense of familiarity with Japan. As a way of promoting friendship with other countries, such modest but steady efforts to introduce Japanese culture abroad should be continued.

Q We've heard that the JET Program, which invites foreign youth as Assistant Language Teachers (ALT) in Japanese junior high and high schools or to work as Coordinators for International Relations (CIR) in local governments, has continued for more than 10 years. We'd like to know what kind of results have been achieved.

The Japan Exchange and Teaching (JET) Program provides Japanese students with opportunities for learning English from Assistant Language Teachers. There is no doubt

An English class
with a JET Program
assistant.

よるコミュニケーション能力が増しているこ
とは疑う余地のないことです。また、各国か
ら参加する青年たちと接する日本の生徒たち
が、海外に対する関心に目覚めたり、海外の
文化を学ぶ良い機会を与えられていることも
事実です。

　また、外国から参加する青年たちにとっ
ても、日本各地のコミュニティーにとけ込ん
で地元の人々と接触することによって、これ
までもっていた日本の文化や社会に対する固
定観念を取り払い、自分自身の体験を通じ
て日本を理解するという、参加青年と生徒
や学校関係者のみならず、周りの人々の異
文化理解の増進に大きく役立っていると言
えます。

　地方自治体の国際交流員の仕事内容は、
自治体によって異なりますが、国際交流事業
の企画立案や実施、国際交流行事、姉妹都
市提携を結んでいる都市との間のコーディネ
ート、外国語文書の翻訳や監修、職員に対
する語学指導などです。こうして国際交流員
は、諸外国と交流を進めている自治体の大
きな力となっています。

　なお、JETプログラムに参加した各国の青
年たちは、帰国後、各地でJETアルムナイ
（OB会）を結成し、各国におけるJETの募
集・選考やそれに先立つ広報に協力をして
くれるケースも増えています。

　また、このJETプログラムに参加した各
国の青年の中には、帰国後、大学院に入学
して日本に関する研究に進んだり、日本と関

that we have seen growing interest in the English language and that students' abilities to communicate in English have improved. Japanese students who communicate with JET participants from around the world tend to show interest in foreign countries, and have opportunities to learn about foreign culture.

Also, as participants from overseas come into contact with local residents and blend into communities throughout Japan, they can eliminate stereotyped images about Japanese culture and society, and come to better appreciate and understand Japan through their own personal experiences. In this important way, the JET Program serves to promote understanding of different cultures not just among the young people from abroad, the Japanese students and others engaged in school-related activities, but more broadly among people in the surrounding communities.

The work of JET Program-sponsored Coordinators for International Relations varies depending upon local governments, but may include planning and execution of international exchange activities, international cultural exchange events, coordination between cities with "sister city" exchange agreements, translating and editing foreign-language written material, and language instruction for local government employees. In such ways, the Coordinators for International Relations are playing an important role in the efforts of local governments to promote exchanges with other countries.

There is a growing number of examples of young people who, having participated in the JET Program, organize, after returning to their home countries, JET alumni clubs which help to make the JET Program better known and help with the recruitment and selection of new JET Program participants.

Some former JET participants on their return home go to graduate schools to take up Japan-related studies or find jobs in Japan-related fields. The JET Program thus contributes

係する仕事につくケースもあります。こうして、JETプログラムは、日本と諸外国の間の広がりある友好親善に貢献しています。

Q 世界各地で日本語を学ぶ人が
増えているようですが、
日本は諸外国での日本語普及のために
どんなことをしていますか。

　　　国際交流基金では、世界各国での日本語普及のため、様々な事業を行っています。たとえば、日本語教師を世界各国の日本語教育機関・教育省に派遣し、派遣先で学生や一般社会人を対象とした日本語講座を開いて教育活動を行ったりしています。また最近では、日本語教育が正規の中等教育へ組み込まれたオーストラリアやニュージーランドには、現地の日本語教師に対し日本語教授法を指導する中等教育アドバイザーの派遣を行っています。

　　　また、各国での日本語教育をサポートするため、大学等の日本語講座の講師の給料を助成したり、日本語学習者による日本語弁論大会の開催経費や賞品等の助成を行ったりもしています。

　　　各国での中学・高校レベルでの日本語教育が拡大する一方では、現地の日本語教師の不足を始めとする様々な問題が生じています。このため国際交流基金では、海外の主要な基金事務所内に「海外日本語センター」を設置し、現地の日本語教師を対象とした日本語教育研修会やセミナー、シンポジウム

to a broad spectrum of positive and friendly relations between Japan and other countries.

Q The number of people studying Japanese throughout the world is increasing. What is Japan doing to promote the Japanese language abroad?

The Japan Foundation carries out several types of activities designed to promote the study of the Japanese language throughout the world. For example, it sends Japanese language instructors to ministries of education and Japanese language educational facilities in other countries. These instructors offer language courses and other educational activities for students and adults who wish to study Japanese. In recent years, the Japan Foundation has been sending intermediate-level educational advisors to give guidance in Japanese teaching methodology to Japanese instructors in Australia and New Zealand, where the study of Japanese has been incorporated into the general curriculum at the intermediate level.

The Japan Foundation also provides financial assistance for Japanese instructors in universities and other institutions and assists with the expenses of holding speech contests for Japanese language students and providing prizes for winners.

With the steady expansion of Japanese language courses at the junior high and high school levels in various countries, many types of problems have arisen, including shortages of local Japanese language teachers. In an effort to overcome such problems, the Japan Foundation has established Overseas Japanese Language Centers in some of its main overseas offices. Activities include seminars, sympo-

の開催を始めとした様々な事業を実施してい
ます。最近の例では、1997年にロンドンに
日本語センターが開設されました。

　総合的な日本語研修センターとしては、各
国の日本語教師の研修を主な目的に、1989
年に埼玉県浦和市に日本語研修センターが
開設されたのを始め、1997年には、大阪の
りんくうタウンに関西国際センターが開設さ
れ、海外の日本語学習の多様なニーズに応
えられるよう基盤づくりが進んでいます。

siums and training courses in Japanese teaching methods for local language instructors. A recent example is the Japanese Language Center opened in London in 1997.

As a comprehensive Japanese language training center, the Japan Language Institute was opened in 1989 in Urawa, Saitama Prefecture, primarily to give training to Japanese language instructors from different countries. The Japanese Language Institute Kansai was established in Rinkū Town, Osaka Prefecture in 1997, and other efforts to build infrastructure to meet the various needs of Japanese language instruction abroad are continuing.

人物紹介

アンコールの
遺跡を
修復する

1992年、UNTAC（国連カンボジア暫定統治機構）の支援のもとに、内戦が続いたカンボジアに平和が訪れました。そして、戦火の中で人が近づくこともできないまま荒れ果てていた古代クメール帝国の貴重な遺跡アンコールに、1994年、やっと修復の手が伸ばされました。その修復チームを率いたのが友田さんでした。

友田さんは中学、高校時代には、日本歴史の研究クラブに入っていました。そして、城や古い寺を回るうちに、次第にそれらの「建築物」としての魅力に取りつかれていきました。

大学は迷わず建築学科に進み、さらに日本の伝統建築、特に中世の密教寺院への興味を深めていきました。大学時代にインド、ネパール、中国、チベットを回って、その風土、歴史、文化の深さ、偉大さに感銘を受け、大学院では建築史の研究に取り組んでいます。

1990年、友田さんは大学院を出て建築設計会社に就職しますが、歴史的な建築物の研究に対する夢は高まるばかりで、休暇ができると、インド、パキスタン、タイ、ミャンマーなどの古い遺跡を訪ね歩きました。

そんな時に大学時代の恩師から、アンコール遺跡群の修復作業の支援のために建築の専門家を、日本政府が探している、とい

**国際交流基金
長期派遣
専門家**
ともだ まさひこ
友田正彦

Tomoda
Masahiko
**Expert on
Long-Term
Japan
Foundation
Assignment**

Helping Restore Angkor Monuments

In 1992, with the help of the United Nations Transitional Authority in Cambodia (UNTAC), peace came to a land that had suffered from long years of civil war. In 1994, work began on restoring the important monuments of Angkor, dating from the ancient Khmer Empire, which had been inaccessible and damaged during the war. Mr. Tomoda became the field manager of a restoration team.

When he was in junior high and high school, Mr. Tomoda had taken part in an extracurricular club that studied Japanese history and culture. By visiting Japanese castles and old temples, he came to be particularly fascinated by works of architecture.

He had no hesitation in choosing architecture as a university major. He continued to cultivate his interest in Japan's traditional architecture, and especially in medieval esoteric Buddhist temples. During his years at the university, he visited India, Nepal, and China (including Tibet), and was deeply impressed by these countries' geographical and historical backgrounds, as well as the greatness and profundity of their cultures. In graduate school he dedicated himself to the study of architectural history.

In 1990. Mr. Tomoda finished his graduate studies and took a job with an architectural design firm, but his dream of doing further research on historical buildings only grew larger. When he had free time he visited historical sites in countries such India, Pakistan, Myanmar, and Thailand.

It was during this period that he heard from a former university teacher that the Japanese government was looking for specialists in architecture to help with the work of restor-

人物紹介

うニュースが伝えられました。友田さんは迷わず、応募することを決心しました。そして、国際交流基金による長期派遣の文化遺産保存専門家として採用されることになったのです。

しかし、統一国家再建の作業に入ったとはいえ、カンボジアの国内の態勢はなかなか整わず、友田さんがカンボジアに入ることができたのは、1994年2月になってからのことでした。

カンボジアでは、なにもかもゼロから準備を始めなければなりませんでした。カンボジア政府の文化芸術省やユネスコ、各国の専門家などとの打ち合わせを重ね、修復の準備のための調査発掘が始まったときは、もう7月になっていました。そして、補修の施工担当者、考古学の専門家などが日本から加わり、本格的な修復作業が軌道に乗り始めたのは、1996年になってからのことでした。

今、アンコール遺跡群の修復作業は、友田さんをはじめ、世界から集められた知恵で、着々と進んでいます。

友田さんは1997年の2月に、ひとまずの役目を終え日本に帰ってきて、今は、主に日本の文化財の修復保護を仕事とする会社に所属しています。そしてそのかたわら、ユネスコからの依頼で、中国の西安にある遺跡「大明宮含元殿」の修復のコンサルタントをしています。

Mr. Tomoda surveying
the Angkor Thom remains

ing the historical sites at Angkor. Without hesitation, Mr. Tomoda decided to apply. As a result he was selected as an architectural specialist to be sent on long-term assignment by the Japan Foundation.

Even though Cambodia was said to have entered a new period of rebuilding a unified country, its internal situation was still rather chaotic and it was not until February 1994 that Mr. Tomoda was able to enter the country.

In Cambodia, preparations for nearly everything had to start from scratch. After several consultations with the Cambodian government's Ministry of Culture and Fine Arts, UNESCO, and international experts at the field, it was not until July that study excavations were begun in preparation for the restoration work. And it was not until 1996 that the restoration work actually got under way with the help of others from Japan, including specialists in archaeology and persons directly responsible for carrying out the needed repairs.

Today the restoration work at Angkor is making steady progress as a result of Mr. Tomoda's help, and knowledge and skills gathered from throughout the world.

Mr. Tomoda completed his Cambodian assignment in February 1997 and returned to Japan, where he is now employed by a company that is mainly engaged in the preservation and restoration of Japan's important cultural properties. Responding to a request from UNESCO, he has become, on the side, a restoration consultant for the Hanyuan Hall at the Daming Palace Site in Xi'an, China.

世界における
人権の促進・民主化の
発展のために

Toward Democratization
and Promotion of
Human Rights

Q 世界ではどのような人権問題が
起こっているのですか。

　　世界には、虐殺や裁判を経ない処刑等に
より命を奪われたり、拷問や裁判を経ない長
期間の拘禁により自由を奪われたり、政治的
意見を表明することを制限されたりしている
人々が数多くいます。

　　また、アフリカのルワンダや旧ユーゴ等に
おける紛争により発生した難民の生命が脅か
されている状況等も国際的に問題とされてい
ます。さらに、女性に対する差別や児童の性
的搾取・虐待の問題もあります。

Healthy, bright-faced children in Cambodia ▲

Q What kinds of human rights problems can we see around the world?

In the world there are significant numbers of people who lose their lives through massacres or capital punishment without trial, who are deprived of their freedom as a result of torture or long-term detention without trial, and who are subject to limitations on their freedom to express political opinions.

Also subject to international scrutiny are situations like those in Rwanda and the former Yugoslavia where the lives of persons who have become refugees as a result of political and military disputes are endangered. Other issues concern discrimination against women or the sexual exploitation and abuse of children.

ルワンダの人権状況

ルワンダでは、1994年4月以降、多数派フツ族と少数派ツチ族との部族対立を背景として1990年10月に始まった内戦の激化にともない、一般民間人の大量殺害や約200万人に上る大量難民の発生など、重大な人権侵害が激増しました。

国連は、同年5月に、ルワンダの人権状況改善のための方策を検討するための人権委員会特別会期を緊急に開催し、その後も、国連総会および人権委員会で決議が採択されています。

93年10月には、国連ルワンダ支援団(UNAMIR)が設立され、新政府樹立支援、停戦監視、治安維持や人道的援助任務にあたっていましたが、96年3月に任務を終え、撤退しました。

94年11月には、国際人道法違反の個人を処罰するためにルワンダ国際刑事裁判所が設置され、現在も活動を続けています。

96年には、大量難民を受け容れていたザイール東部地域において少数民族問題に端を発する紛争が激化し、100万人を超えるルワンダ難民が影響を被りました。また、混乱の中で、大量の難民の帰還が実現したものの、民族大量虐殺容疑者を巡る暴力事件の多発など、まだまだ多くの課題が残されています。

日本は、同国における人権状況の改善のために、同国における国連人権高等弁務官事務所の人権監視活動に対し70万ドルを拠出しています。人権侵害や民主的政権の不在等により、ODA大綱の原則に照らして停

Human Rights Situation in Rwanda

After April 1994, as a result of the intensification of the civil war which started in October 1990 out of tribal antagonisms between the majority Hutu ethnic group and the minority Tutsi ethnic group, Rwanda saw a steep increase in serious human rights violations including mass killings of ordinary citizens and the creation of some 2 million refugees.

In May 1994, the United Nations, as an emergency measure, opened a special session of the UN Commission on Human Rights to investigate ways of improving the Rwandan human rights situation, and resolutions have been adopted by the United Nations General Assembly and the Commission since then.

The United Nations Assistance Mission for Rwanda (UNAMIR) was set up in October 1993 to support the establishment of a new government, monitor a truce, maintain order, and give humanitarian aid. It withdrew from Rwanda after ending its duties in March 1996.

In November 1994, the International Criminal Tribunal for Rwanda was established to punish individuals convicted of violating international humanitarian laws, and it continues its activities at present.

In 1996, hostilities worsened as a result of problems among minority ethnic groups in the eastern part of Zaire, which had accepted a large number of refugees from Rwanda, and over 1 million Rwandan refugees were affected. Even in the midst of such confusion, large numbers of refugees were repatriated, but a great many problems are still unresolved.

In order to improve the human rights situation in Rwanda, Japan has contributed 700 thousand US dollars for human rights monitoring activities of the United Nations Rwanda Office of the High Commissioner for Human Rights. Though Japan had cut off its economic cooperation in accor-

止していた経済協力についても、96年7月
に派遣した調査団の結果を踏まえ、ルワンダ
国民の基礎的な生活にかかわる分野を中心
に協力を検討していくこととしています。

ミャンマーの人権状況

また、ミャンマーでは、1988年に民主化
要求運動が発生し、同年9月の軍による全権
掌握を背景に、人権侵害の問題があるとし
て、国際的な非難を受けています。拷問、強
制労働、強制移住、政治的理由による逮
捕・拘禁、表現・集会の自由を含む基本的
自由の制限、少数民族に対する抑圧、正規
の裁判を経ない処刑などが行われているとい
うのです。

この問題は、国連では90年以降、国連人
権委員会で取り上げられており、91年から
は総会でも毎年取り上げられ、人権問題に関
する決議が採択されています。ミャンマーの
民主化運動の指導者でノーベル平和賞を受賞
したアウン・サン・スー・チーさんが、95
年に、軍事政権による自宅軟禁から6年ぶり
に解放されましたが、これにより事態が大き
な改善を見せているわけではありません。

日本は、ミャンマーを国際政治の中で孤立
させるのではなく、同国政府との対話を維持
し、同国を国際社会により開かれたものとす
るとともに、民主化、人権状況の改善につい
て前向きな動きを促進すべく働きかけていま
す。また、同時に、民主化および人権状況
の改善を見守りつつ、継続している案件や、
ミャンマー国民に直接役立つ基礎生活分野

dance with the principles of its ODA Charter (due to human rights violations and the absence of a democratic regime), it has been decided, on the basis of the results of a survey mission sent in July 1996, to explore the possibility of resuming economic cooperation, especially in fields directly related to the basic daily-life needs of the Rwandan people.

Human Rights Situation in Myanmar

In Myanmar, a movement demanding democratization appeared in 1988 and, as a result of the takeover of power by the country's armed forces in September of that year, there was much international criticism alleging violations of human rights. The allegations referred to torture, forced labor, forced relocation, arrest and confinement for political reasons, restriction on fundamental human rights including freedoms of expression and assembly, oppression of minority ethnic groups, and executions without process of trial.

These problems have been taken up since 1990 by the UN Commission on Human Rights, and have been taken up every year since 1991 by the General Assembly, where human rights resolutions have been adopted. In 1995, Aung San Suu Kyi, who is a leader of Myanmar's democratization movement and a Nobel Peace Prize winner, was released from six years of home confinement by the military government, but this alone has not brought any great improvement to the human rights scene.

Japan is trying to maintain a dialogue with the government of Myanmar, rather than isolate Myanmar in international politics. Moreover, Japan is appealing to the government of Myanmar to become more open to international society, and to advocate that it hasten progressive trends toward democratization and improvements in its human rights record. At the same time, while paying attention to democratization and improvements in human rights, after due study and consideration, Japan is trying

に関わる案件を中心に経済協力を検討の上、実施していくこととしています。

Q

国全体として経済的に発展することが、1人1人の人権を守ることに優先するという考え方があります。このように経済発展と人権とは対立するものなのでしょうか。

現在、人権問題は南北対立の様相をも示しており、思想・良心、表現、集会・結社の自由等をはじめとする市民的・政治的権利(自由権的基本権)の重要性を主張する西側諸国に対して、まずは貧困から脱することが先決であり、そのためにはこうした権利のある程度の制約もやむを得ないとして、「生存権」や経済的・社会的権利をより重視する開発途上国の間で対立があります。

人権に、市民的・政治的権利と経済的・社会的権利の両面があり、双方とも大切なことは、それぞれの国際規約÷1があることからも明らかです。従って、人が貧困から脱し健康で文化的な生活を営めることが重要であることは言うまでもありませんが、同時に、経済的発展の重要性を理由として、人権(自由権的基本権)をないがしろにすることも認められるものではありません。

注1 国際人権規約 国連は1948年に、人権保障の標準を示すものとして「世界

to carry out economic cooperation projects, particularly ongoing long-range projects and types of assistance which have a direct bearing on the basic human needs of Myanmar's people.

Q Some people think that developing the economy of a country as a whole should take priority over protection of each individual's human rights.
Are economic development and human rights in conflict?

At present, human rights issues show aspects of North-South opposition. Western European countries emphasize the importance of civil and political rights relating to thought, conscience, expression, assembly and association (i.e., freedom-related fundamental rights). On the other hand, some developing countries place a greater emphasis on "rights to live" and other economic and social rights, with the reasoning that priority should be given to efforts to free themselves from poverty and that the other rights must for that purpose be, to some extent, restricted.

There are two aspects of human rights—one civil and political rights, and the other, economic and social rights— and both are important as they are codified in respective International Covenants. ❖1 Thus, while it is obvious that it is essential for human beings to cast off poverty and lead healthy and cultured lives, it is not acceptable to neglect other human rights (i.e., freedom-related fundamental rights) by reason of the importance of economic development.

NOTE 1 International Covenants on Human Rights — The United Nations in 1948 adopted the Universal Declaration of Human Rights,

人権宣言」を採択したが、これは法的拘束力を持つものではなかった。そこでこれを条約化し、実施を義務づけたものが国際人権規約である。経済的、社会的および文化的権利に関する規約(A規約)と、市民的および政治的権利に関する規約(B規約)の2規約に分かれ、さらに後者に関する選択議定書がある。1976年に発効。

Q 人権の保障のために、国際社会はどのような取り組みをしていますか。

　人権問題は、国際社会が取り組んでいる外交の重要な一分野です。国連憲章において国連の目的の1つとして人権尊重がうたわれ、1948年の世界人権宣言、1976年の国際人権規約といった人権に関する基本的文書・条約が採択・締結されてきました。

　1993年6月には、ウィーンにおいて、171の国家が参加し、約1500のNGOから3000人以上がオブザーバーとして出席して、1968年のテヘラン会議についで2回目の世界人権会議が開催されました。ここでは、「ウィーン宣言及び行動計画」が採択され、人権が普遍的価値であることや、人権が国際社会の正当な関心事であることなどが確認されました。
　また、同会議での討議を踏まえ、同年12月の国連総会において、人権高等弁務官の設置が決定されました。人権高等弁務官は、

which indicates standards for the protection of human rights but is not itself legally binding. The International Covenants on Human Rights put its provisions into treaty form, and impose the duty of implementation on member states, making their exercise legally binding. There are two covenants: the International Covenant on Economic, Social and Cultural Rights (known as Protocol A) and the International Covenant on Civil and Political Rights (known as Protocol B). There is also an "Optional Protocol," related to the latter. The Covenants came into effect in 1976.

Q What sorts of measures are being taken by international society for the protection of human rights?

Human rights issues are an essential part of the diplomatic activities of international society. In the Charter of the United Nations, respect for human rights is mentioned as one of the purposes of the United Nations. Such basic documents and treaties on human rights as the Universal Declaration of Human Rights in 1948 and the International Covenants on Human Rights in 1976 were adopted .

In June 1993, the second World Conference on Human Rights (following the first conference held in Tehran in 1968) was held in Vienna with the participation of 171 countries and over 3,000 observers from approximately 1,500 NGOs. At this conference, the Vienna Declaration and Program of Action was adopted, recognizing human rights as of universal value and a legitimate concern of the international community.

Based on the discussions carried out at this Vienna Conference, it was decided in the United Nations General Assembly, in December 1993, to establish a High Commi-

国連の人権分野における諸活動を総括することとなっており、その任務には、すべての市民的・文化的・経済的・政治的および社会的権利の効果的享受の促進と保護、人権に関わる諸機関への勧告、政府との対話、国連人権高等弁務官事務所の監督、総会への年次報告の提出などが含まれます。現在の国連人権高等弁務官(UNHCHR)は、メアリー・ロビンソン前アイルランド大統領です。

また、欧州、米州、アフリカ地域においては、人権擁護に関するそれぞれの地域の協力機構が設立されており、地域ごとに人権を擁護・促進しようとする努力が行われています。

Q 人権問題に関する活動を行っている国際的な機関・団体にはどのようなものがありますか。

人権問題に関する活動を行っている国際的な機関としては、国連人権高等弁務官事務所および種々の人権メカニズムがあり、国連人権委員会の決議等に基づき世界各地で問題になっている人権侵害の調査や報告を行っています。さらに人権問題について各国が話し合いを進める場として国連総会(第3委員会)および国連人権委員会等があります。後者は、地理的に公平に振り分けられた53ヵ国の代表によりなっており、日本は1982年以降メンバー国です。

また、同委員会が国家代表で構成される

ssioner for Human Rights, who coordinates various activities of the United Nations in the human rights field. The duties of the High Commissioner include promoting and protecting the effective enjoyment of all civil, cultural, economic, political and social rights, making recommendations to the various bodies concerned with human rights, engaging in a dialogue with governments, overall supervision of the Office of the United Nations High Commissioner for Human Rights (UNHCHR), and submitting annual reports to the General Assembly. The current High Commissioner for Human Rights is the former President of Ireland, Mrs. Mary Robinson.

Efforts are also made on a regional basis to protect and promote human rights, and mechanisms for regional human rights protection have been set up in Europe, the Americas, and Africa.

Q What sorts of international organizations and groups carry out activities related to human rights issues?

International bodies concerned with human rights issues include the Office of the United Nations High Commissioner for Human Rights and the various human rights mechanisms which it represents. They carry out investigations and submit reports, based on resolutions of the UN Commission on Human Rights, of alleged human rights violations throughout the world. Other forums where countries can carry out discussions on human rights issues include the UN General Assembly (Third Committee) and the UN Commission on Human Rights. The latter is composed of representatives of 53 countries which are elected in a geographically fair manner. Japan has been a member since 1982.

While the UN Commission on Human Rights is com-

のに対して、同委員会の下部組織として、個人の資格で選ばれるメンバーからなる人権小委員会(「差別防止及び少数者保護小委員会」)があります。同小委員会では、人権に関する研究や、人種、民族、宗教および言語における少数派の人権の保護に関して国連人権委員会に勧告すること、経済社会理事会および人権委員会から委任された任務を行っています。

さらに、これらとは別に、人権関係の各条約の規定に基づき、締約国の報告を受け、それについて審議する機関として設けられた委員会(規約人権委員会、女子差別撤廃委員会、児童の権利委員会等)があります。

また、NGOも数多く活躍しています。もっとも大きな団体としては、アムネスティ・インターナショナル✢2が有名です。

注2 アムネスティ・インターナショナル (Amnesty International)
1961年創設の民間の国際的人権擁護組織。Amnestyは特赦の意味。思想や信条、皮膚の色、言語、民族、宗教上の理由で投獄された非暴力の人々の釈放、すべての死刑・拷問への反対、政治犯に対する公正・迅速な裁判の実施、などを求めて活動している。本部はロンドン。日本にも支部がある。

posed of representatives of states, a human rights sub-commission, namely the Sub-Commission on Prevention of Discrimination and Protection of Minorities, which is a subordinate organization to the Commission on Human Rights, is composed of members elected according to individual competence. This sub-commission undertakes duties allotted to it by the Economic and Social Council and by the UN Commission on Human Rights, along with such activities as conducting human rights studies and making recommendations to the Commission on Human Rights on the protection of the rights of racial, ethnic, religious and linguistic minorities.

Apart from these mechanisms, based on the provisions of human rights instruments, UN committees have been established which receive and consider reports from member states. Among them are the Human Rights Committee, the Committee on the Elimination of Discrimination against Women, and the Committee on the Rights of the Child.

A large number of NGOs are also active in this field. Amnesty International ❖2 is widely known as the largest among them.

NOTE 2 Amnesty International is an international NGO for the protection of human rights, founded in 1961. "Amnesty" means "special pardon." The organization is active in demanding the release of non-violent persons who have been imprisoned for reasons of thought or belief, color of skin, language, ethnicity, or religion. It is opposed to all death penalties and torture, and demands the holding of fair and prompt trials for persons accused of political offenses. Its headquarters is located in London and there is a branch in Japan.

Q 日本は国際的な人権問題に対して、どのように取り組んでいるのでしょうか。

　日本政府の人権問題への取り組みとしては、第一に国連の活動への協力があります。

　人権委員会のメンバー国として国際社会における人権議論を積極的にリードしているほか、人権高等弁務官事務所が中心となる諸活動に対する資金協力として、1996年度には、人権関係の自発的基金に年間118万ドルを拠出しています。また、ルワンダにおける人権高等弁務官事務所による人権監視活動に、これまで70万ドル、旧ユーゴスラビアにおける人権フィールドオペレーションに、これまで80万ドルを拠出しています。

　さらに、差別防止および少数者保護小委員会、B規約人権委員会、女子差別撤廃委員会等、国連の各種委員会において、波多野里望氏(学習院大学教授)、横田洋三氏(東京大学教授)、安藤仁介氏(同志社大学教授)、多谷千香子氏(大阪高等検察庁検事)ら日本人委員が活躍するなど、人的にも貢献しています。

　国連以外での活動としては、1996年のリヨン・サミットにおいて「民主的発展のためのパートナーシップ：PDD：Partnership for Democratic Development」計画を発表しました。人権状況の改善に努力している開発途上国に対し、その民主的発展のための制度づくり・人づくりを支援しています。

　さらに、1992年に閣議決定された「政府

Q How is Japan dealing with international human rights issues?

One of the most important ways in which the Japanese government is involved in human rights issues is cooperation with the activities of the United Nations.

Besides exercising active leadership in international discussions on human rights issues as a member of the United Nations Commission on Human Rights, Japan gives financial support for the activities of the Office of the High Commissioner for Human Rights (OHCHR). Japan's contributions to Voluntary Funds for human rights activities amounted to 1.18 million dollars in fiscal 1996. To date, Japan has provided 700 thousand dollars for human rights monitoring activities by the OHCHR in Rwanda, and 800 thousand dollars for human rights "field operations" in the former Yugoslavia.

As for human resource contributions, Japanese are active in various UN committees including the Sub-Commission on Prevention of Discrimination and Protection of Minorities, the Protocol B Human Rights Committee on Civil and Political Rights, and the Committee on the Elimination of Discrimination against Women. Among Japanese members are Hatano Ribot (Professor of Gakushūin University), Yokota Yōzō (Professor of the University of Tokyo), Andō Nisuke (Professor of Dōshisha University), and Taya Chikako (Public Prosecutor at the Osaka High Public Prosecutor's Office).

An example of Japanese activities outside the United Nations framework is the Partnership for Democratic Development (PDD) plan announced at the 1996 Lyon Summit. This plan provides assistance for the training of personnel and the building of systems for democratic development in developing countries that are making efforts toward improving human rights situations.

In Japan's Official Development Assistance Charter,

開発援助大綱(ODA大綱)」において、開発途上国への援助に際しては、人権の保障状況につき注意を払う旨を明記しています。

また、アジア太平洋地域における人権の擁護・促進のための協力を話し合うことを目的として、95年、96年、98年には外務省と国連大学が共催で「アジア太平洋人権シンポジウム」を開催しています。

Q 民主化が、現在、いろいろな地域で進んでいるようですが、実態はどのようなものでしょうか。

民主化は人権の擁護にとって不可欠です。現在、世界のいろいろな地域で民主化が進んでいますが、いまだ民主体制が脆弱なところも少なくありません。

アジアでは、カンボジアにおいて、長年の内戦にピリオドが打たれ、1993年には、国連カンボジア暫定統治機構(UNTAC)の管理下、制憲議会選挙が行われ、シアヌーク国王を元首とした立憲君主政府が発足しました。しかし、98年の総選挙を控えた2大政党間の軋轢の高まりを背景に情勢が不安定になり、97年7月にはプノンペンにおいて2大政党間で武力衝突が発生しました。その後事態は鎮静化し、現在カンボジア政府では、98年7月26日に自由・公正な選挙が実施されました。

中南米では、キューバを除くすべての国が民主体制に移行しています。グアテマラでは、96年12月、36年間続いた中米地域に

approved by cabinet resolution in 1992, it is clearly stated that in providing assistance to developing countries attention is to be paid to the degree to which human rights are supported and protected.

With the purpose of discussing cooperative efforts to protect and promote human rights in the Asia-Pacific region, the Ministry of Foreign Affairs sponsored, jointly with the United Nations University, a Symposium on Human Rights in the Asia-Pacific Region, in 1995, 1996, and 1998.

Q It seems that democratization is currently ongoing in many regions, but what are some of the actual situations?

Democratization is indispensable for the protection of human rights. At present, democratization is ongoing in various regions in the world, but there are still many places where democratic structures are weak.

As for Asia, long years of civil war in Cambodia were brought to an end, and elections for a parliament to establish a constitution were held in 1993 under the supervision of the United Nations Transitional Authority in Cambodia (UNTAC). As a result, a constitutional monarchy, with King Sihanouk as head of state, began functioning. However, the situation again became unstable with growing frictions between the two main political parties in the period leading up to the general elections scheduled for 1998, and armed clashes occurred between the two main political parties in Phnom Penh in July 1997. The situation later calmed down, and the government of Cambodia held a free and fair election on July 26, 1998.

In Latin America, all countries with the exception of Cuba have adopted democratic systems. In Guatemala a peace agreement was signed in December 1996, putting an end to a

おける最後の内戦に終止符を打つ和平合意が署名されました。また、94年に軍政から民政に移行したハイチでは、選挙を経て96年2月に就任したプレバル大統領の下、民主体制の定着のための努力が行われています。

アフリカでは、94年7月以降軍事政権が続いていたガンビアで、96年8月に新改正憲法の国民投票および9月に大統領選挙が行われました。

日本は、96年のリヨン・サミットにおいて「民主的発展のためのパートナーシップ：PDD」計画を発表しました。これは、民主化や人権状況の改善に努力しながらもそのための制度や人材を欠いている国々に対し、法制度や選挙制度の整備、司法官・警察官の研修などの支援、技術協力を、2国間あるいは多国間の援助を通じて、より積極的かつ総合的に実施しようとするものです。

また96年には、アジアではバングラデシュ、ガザおよびヨルダン川西岸の選挙に、また、ラテン・アメリカではグアテマラとニカラグア、ヨーロッパではボスニア・ヘルツェゴビナに、選挙監視要員を派遣するなど、各地の民主化プロセスの支援を行っています。

Q 民主化のための選挙に国際的な監視団が派遣されることが多くなってきていますが、このような監視団には日本からどのような人が参加しているのですか。

日本は、これまで約60の選挙に延べ約400名の選挙監視要員を派遣しています。こ

civil war that had continued for 36 years. And in Haiti, which moved from a military to a civilian government in 1994, efforts to permanently establish a democratic system are being carried out under the guidance of President René Preval who became the country's head of state following elections in February 1996.

In Gambia, West Africa, where a military government continued in power from July 1994, a referendum on a revised draft constitution was held in August 1996, and a presidential election took place in September.

As mentioned earlier, at the 1996 Lyon Summit, Japan introduced a plan called Partnership for Democratic Development (PDD). This plan outlines a more positive and comprehensive provision of support and technical cooperation, on both a bilateral and multilateral basis, in such areas as improvement of legal and electoral systems and the training of judicial and police personnel in countries that have lacked infrastructure and personnel in these fields but are making efforts toward democratization and improving human rights.

Japan is also assisting processes of democratization around the world, for example, by sending electoral observers in 1996 for elections to help with elections in Gaza, the West Bank, and Bangladesh in Asia; Guatemala and Nicaragua in Latin America; and Bosnia-Herzegovina in Europe.

Q It is becoming more common for international monitoring teams to be sent to help with elections for democratization, but who from Japan is taking part?

Japan has up to now sent a total of approximately 400 electoral observers to help with approximately 60 elections

のうち、国連PKOには、89年10月のナミ
ビアに27名をはじめとして、アンゴラ(国連
第2次アンゴラ検証団)、カンボジア(国連カ
ンボジア暫定統治機構)、モザンビーク(国連
モザンビーク活動)およびエルサルバドル(国
連エルサルバドル監視団)の各選挙に、延べ
116名を派遣しています。

　これら選挙要員は、投票行動を監視する
など選挙の監視を担当する選挙監視要員と、
投票所の設営を監督するなど選挙の運営を
担当する選挙管理要員に大別されます。

　この選挙監視要員および選挙管理要員に
求められる資質としては、選挙監視・管理そ
の他関連業務の経験、英語等言語能力、判
断能力、選挙支援チームの一員として様々な
文化環境の中で業務を行い生活できる能力お
よび覚悟、身体的健康等が挙げられていま
す。
　日本からはこれまで、国会議員や国家公
務員および地方自治体職員はもちろん、会
社員、仕事を1ヵ月休業してきた自営業、ボ
ランティア問題を教える大学教授、国際関
係論を専攻する大学院生、著述業、記者、
難民問題に長年携わってきたNGO関係者な
ど幅広い層から延べ400人が選挙要員とし
て参加しています。

abroad. Among these, 116 were dispatched to help with elections held as a part of United Nations Peacekeeping Operations (PKO). These include 27 Japanese personnel sent to Namibia in October 1989 and others sent to Angola (as part of the Second UN Angola Verification Mission), Cambodia (with the UN Transitional Authority in Cambodia), Mozambique (with the UN Operation in Mozambique), and El Salvador (with the UN Observer Mission in El Salvador).

These electoral observers consist of two categories of personnel, one being election monitoring personnel responsible for observing polling activities, and the other being election supervisory personnel responsible for supervising the setting up of polling stations and other important aspects of planning for elections.

Qualities looked for in the selection of these electoral observers include prior experience with election monitoring or supervision, English and other language abilities, good judgment, good health, and ability and willingness to live in various cultural environments while carrying out their duties as members of the electoral assistance teams.

Up until now, approximately 400 Japanese from a wide variety of backgrounds have participated in such work. They include members of the Diet and employees of the national and local governments, but also company employees, self-employed persons who have taken a month off from their regular work, university professors who teach about volunteer issues, graduate students specializing in international relations, writers, journalists, and members of NGOs that have long been concerned with refugee issues.

Q 女性の権利問題とはどのようなものですか。女性の人権を保障するために、国際社会ではどのような取り組みがなされていますか。

1995年9月、女性の地位向上を目的として、ナイロビ世界会議以来10年ぶりに、第4回世界女性会議が北京において開催され、「北京宣言」と「行動綱領」が採択されました。

宣言では、女性の権利を基本的人権と位置付け、男女平等の推進とあらゆる分野への女性の全面的参加、エンパワーメントなど38項目がうたわれています。

また、行動綱領では、12の重大問題領域(貧困、教育と訓練、健康、暴力、武力紛争、経済、権力および意思決定、地位向上のための制度的仕組み、人権、メディア、環境、女児)を指摘し、これらの分野において2000年に向けて各国、国連などが採るべき措置や行動などが示されました。

行動綱領は、ジェンダー(社会的文化的性別)やリプロダクティブ・ヘルス(性と生殖に関する健康)∻3などの女性の権利が取り入れられています。これらのある概念については、いくつかの宗教的諸国などからの反発が目立ちました。

注3 リプロダクティブ・ヘルス
(性と生殖に関する健康)
1994年9月の国連の国際人口・開発会議
で採択された「今後20年の行動計画」

Q What are "women's rights issues"?
What sorts of measures are being undertaken by the international community to ensure the rights of women?

The Fourth World Conference on Women was held in Beijing in September 1995, ten years after the Nairobi World Conference on Women, for the purpose of further advancing the status of women. It adopted the Beijing Declaration and a Platform for Action.

In its 38 paragraphs, the Beijing Declaration identifies women's rights as human rights and addresses other issues such as promoting equality between women and men, empowerment and full participation of women.

The Platform for Action identifies twelve critical areas of concern, i.e., women and poverty, education and training of women, women and health, violence against women, women and armed conflicts, women and the economy, women in power and decision-making, institutional mechanisms for the advancement of women, human rights of women, women and the media, women and the environment, and the girl child. It points out actions and measures to be taken toward the year 2000 by governments, the United Nations, and others.

The Platform for Action included issues of social and cultural discrimination on the basis of gender, as well as such areas of women's rights as reproductive health ❖3. With respect to some of these concepts, opposition from several religion-oriented countries became evident.

NOTE 3 reproductive health — In the Program of Action for the Coming 20 Years (also called the "Cairo Declaration") adopted by the International Conference on Population and Development in September 1994, the concept of "reproductive health and

(カイロ文書)の中でリプロダクティブ・ヘルス／ライツ(性と生殖に関する健康／権利)という概念がうたわれた。身体的、精神的、社会的に良好な状態で、安全で満足な性生活を営めること、子どもを産むかどうか、産むならばいつ、何人産むかを決定する自由を持つことをいう。同会議では、人口問題の解決には、女性の教育や健康、地位向上により自己決定権が保障されることが不可欠であるという考え方が提唱された。

Q 女性の人権については、文化・宗教・国・地域により考え方が違うと言われますが、どのように違うのでしょうか。

　　一部の国々の中には、文化的、伝統的、宗教的価値を重視するあまり、女性の人権への侵害に結びついているような主張を行う場合があります。確かに、各国にとってこれらの価値は重要ですが、だからといって、人権を不当に侵害して良いという理由にはなりません。

　　ウィーン宣言および行動計画❖4は、国および地域の特殊性、様々な歴史的、文化的および宗教的背景の重要性には留意しつつも、政治的、経済的および文化的システムのいかんを問わず、すべての人権および基本的自由を促進および擁護することが国家の義務である、としています。

　　このような侵害の代表的な例としては、女性性器切除(FGM=Female Genital Mutila-

rights" was emphasized. It calls for women's rights to a safe and satisfying sex life and an individual woman's freedom to decide whether or not to give birth and, if she decides to do so, when and how many children to have under conditions that are favorable to bodily health, mental health, and society. At the Cairo conference, it was emphasized that as a solution to the population problem it is indispensable that rights of self-determination be supported by promotion of women's education and health and the advancement of the status of women in general.

Q It is said that ways of thinking about women's human rights differ according to culture, religion, country, and region. How are they different?

In some countries, there are many who express opinions which, often reflecting a great emphasis on traditional, cultural or religious values, sometimes lead to violations of women's human rights. It is of course true that in these countries such values are important, but this should not be considered a reason to unjustly violate human rights.

In the Vienna Declaration and Program of Action ❖4, it is stated that while the significance of national and regional particularities and various historical, cultural and religious backgrounds must be borne in mind, it is the duty of States, regardless of their political, economic and cultural system, to promote and protect all human rights and fundamental freedoms.

A notable example of violations of women's human rights is female genital mutilation (FGM). This dates back more

tion)があります。これは、アフリカ、中近東、アジアの一部で、1000年以上前から、女性の身体の清浄と節操の証しとして少女に対して行われてきた習慣で、もっとも多いのはクリトリス全体と外陰部を切除するものです。国連人口基金によれば、現在約1億人以上の女性が対象とされてきており、毎年約200万人が受けていると推測されています。

1995年に北京で開催された第4回世界女性会議の行動綱領では、女性器の切除やその他女性に有害な伝統的習慣は、「女性に対する暴力」であるとして明記されています。そして行動綱領は、各国政府が採るべき行動として、女性に対する暴力を非難し、「女性に対する暴力撤廃宣言」(93年国連総会にて採択)に述べられた暴力廃絶に関する自国の義務を、慣習、伝統または宗教的配慮を理由に回避しないこと、としています。

注4 ウィーン宣言および行動計画 1993年3月ウィーンで開催された国連世界人権会議において採択された。

 Q 日本は、国際社会において女性の人権問題に対して、どのように取り組んでいるのでしょうか。

日本は、1958年よりほぼ継続して国連婦人の地位委員会のメンバー国であるほか、国連婦人開発基金(UNIFEM)に対し82年以降継続的に資金拠出を行っています。96年に

than 1,000 years in parts of Africa, the Middle East, and Asia, where it has been customarily performed on young girls with the idea that it is a sign of the purity and chastity of a woman's body. Its most common form is the removal of the entire clitoris and other external features of the genital area. According to the United Nations Population Fund, at present more than 100 million women have had such operations performed on them, and it is estimated that every year approximately 2 million girls are still made to undergo them.

In the Platform for Action adopted at the Fourth World Conference on Women held in Beijing in 1995, the removal of female sexual organs and other traditional customs that are harmful to women are clearly identified as "violence against women." The Platform for Action states that every government must take actions to condemn violence against women and must not, because of considerations of custom, tradition, or religion, neglect its duties to eliminate such violence. This is made clear in the Declaration on the Elimination of Violence Against Women adopted by the UN General Assembly in 1993.

NOTE 4 The Vienna Declaration and Program of Action were adopted by the World Conference on Human Rights held in Vienna in March 1993.

Q How is Japan engaged in women's human rights issues in international society?

Almost continuously since 1958, Japan has been a member of the UN Commission on the Status of Women, and since 1982 Japan has continuously provided financial assistance to the United Nations Development Fund for

は200万ドルを拠出しました。

また、国際婦人調査訓練研修所(INSTRAW)に対し、86年より毎年8万ドルを拠出しています。さらに、第4回世界女性会議のフォローアップの一環として、96年には、女性に対する暴力撤廃のための国連婦人開発基金信託基金に対し資金を拠出しました。

また、女子差別撤廃委員会の委員として日本人では多谷千香子氏が活躍しています。

Q 日本は、開発途上国の女性の健康および教育のために、どのような貢献をしていますか。

国連にはWID (Women in Development：開発における女性の役割)という考え方があります。援助の際に、開発における女性の役割や地位の重要性を認識していこうというものです。

日本は、国連など国際社会の動向を踏まえながらWIDを推進してきました。日本の援助方針を定めたODA大綱の中では、援助を効果的に実施するための方策として、開発への女性の積極的参加と、開発による女性への受益の確保について十分配慮することが挙げられています。

1995年の第4回世界女性会議(於：北京)で日本は「WIDイニシアティブ」を発表し、

Women (UNIFEM). Japan's contribution to the fund in 1996 was 2 million dollars.

Japan has also been providing an annual contribution of 80 thousand dollars since 1986 to the International Research and Training Institute for the Advancement of Women (INSTRAW). As a part of the follow-up activities related to the Fourth World Conference on Women, Japan in 1996 provided financing for a UNIFEM trust fund to support actions aimed at eliminating violence against women.

Ms. Taya Chikako is currently a member of the UN's Committee on the Elimination of Discrimination against Women.

Q What contributions is Japan making to the health and education of women in developing countries?

The United Nations is promoting the concept of "Women in Development" (WID) in relation to assistance to women in developing countries. This concept promotes efforts to recognize, as a part of development assistance projects, the ways in which women's roles and status are essential to the success of development work.

Japan has promoted this WID concept in keeping with trends in the United Nations and other sectors of international society. In the ODA Charter, which specifies the policy underlying Japan's assistance efforts, it is stated that to insure that these assistance efforts are effectively carried out, proper attention is to be given to the active participation of women in development work as well as to insuring that women are adequately benefited through development projects.

At the Fourth World Conference on Women held in Beijing in 1995, Japan announced its WID Initiative. It made

女性の教育、健康、経済・社会活動への参加という3つの分野を中心とした、開発援助でのWID分野の拡充に努力することを明らかにしました。これを具体化するため、外務省、国際協力事業団(JICA)、海外経済協力基金(OECF)では担当部局の設置、ガイドライン作成などを行っています。

また、女性のための職業訓練所の整備、母子保健・家族計画への協力、女子の労働軽減を配慮した井戸掘り、女性分野の行政官の育成など、女性の参加と受益を配慮したプロジェクトを実施してきています。さらに、援助を行うに当たっての事前調査にジェンダー分析を行える専門家を参加させるとともに、援助対象地域の女性の意見を聞くなど、個々の案件の実施過程でも配慮を行うようにしています。

さらに、開発途上国における人口問題や深刻化するエイズ問題に対し、日本は、人口・エイズ問題は人類共通の問題であるとして、1994年2月に「人口・エイズに関する地球規模問題イニシアティブ」を打ち出しました。これは、1994年度から2000年度までの7年間で、ODA総額30億ドルをめどに、途上国に対し積極的にこの分野での協力を進めるというものです。

この推進に当たっては、人口・家族計画や母子保健といった直接的な分野のほか、女性と子どもの健康にかかわる基礎保健医療、初等教育、女性の識字教育・職業訓練など間接的な分野を含めて包括的に取り組むこ

clear its intention to work to expand the WID aspects of its development assistance, concentrating on three fields, namely, women's education, good health, and participation in economic and social activities. To work on the specifics of this initiative, the Ministry of Foreign Affairs, the Japan International Cooperation Agency (JICA), and the Overseas Economic Cooperation Fund (OECF) have set up special departments and have prepared guidelines on the relevant issues.

Among projects being carried out with a view to women's benefits and participation are: the improvement of work training centers for women, cooperation in family planning and mother-child health projects, the digging of wells which reduce the burden borne by women and children in carrying water from distant locations, and the training of administrative personnel whose work is related to women's issues. In the process of carrying out such projects, attention is given to seeing that preliminary studies include the carrying out of "gender analyses" by persons specialized in that field and listening to the ideas and opinions of women in the locations to which the assistance is directed.

With respect to population growth problems and worsening AIDS problems in developing countries, Japan, animated by the recognition that population and AIDS issues are shared by the whole of humankind, put forth in February 1994 its "Global Issues Initiative on Population and AIDS." The Initiative envisages active cooperation with developing countries in these fields over 7 years (from fiscal 1994 through fiscal 2000) and total ODA expenditures of 3 billion dollars.

In pursuing the Initiative's objectives, comprehensive measures are to be taken not only in fields that are directly linked to women's issues like population and family planning, or to maternal and child health, but also in indirectly related fields. These will include basic health care and medical treat-

とにしています。また、実施に当たっては、国際機関やNGOとも連携していくことにしています。

Q いま世界で起こっている子どもの人権問題とはどのようなものですか? 子どもの人権を守るために国際社会、日本はどのような取り組みをしていますか?

世界では今日でも伝染病や栄養失調により毎年多くの子どもたちが亡くなっています。また、紛争などの際には、社会の中でもっとも弱い立場にある子どもたちが大きな被害を受けます。

国際社会における子どもに関する取り組みを行っている機関として、国連児童基金(ユニセフ)があります。ユニセフは主として開発途上国の児童に対し直接援助を与えることを目的として、健康衛生活動や教育・職業訓練を行うもので、児童の権利の保護、基本的必要の充足、能力の完全な育成を任務としています。

また、1989年には国連総会で「児童の権利に関する条約」が採択されました。これは、すべての児童の保護と基本的人権の尊重を促進することを目的としています。日本は、1990年に署名、94年に批准しました。

90年には、ユニセフが事務局となり、71ヵ国の首脳が参加して「子どものための世界サミット」が開催されました。同サミットでは、

ment of women and children, elementary education, and work training and literacy education for women. To help achieve these aims, efforts are being made to cooperate with international bodies and NGOs.

Q In today's world, what kind of human rights issues exist in relation to children? What measures are Japan and the international community taking to protect the rights of the child?

In many parts of the world, large numbers of children still die every year as a result of infectious diseases and/or malnutrition. Also, in cases of armed conflict, children, who are in the weakest position in society, suffer immense harm.

The United Nations Children's Fund (UNICEF) is the foremost organization in the international community that is concerned primarily with children's issues. UNICEF's purpose is to provide direct assistance to children, especially in the developing countries. It carries out activities in the fields of health and hygiene as well as educational and work training projects. It is entrusted with the protection of children's rights, fulfillment of children's basic needs, and activities aiming at the full development of children's abilities.

In 1989, the Convention on the Rights of the Child was adopted at the United Nations General Assembly. Its purpose is to further the protection of all children and respect for their fundamental human rights. Japan signed the Convention in 1990 and ratified it in 1994.

In 1990, the World Summit for Children, organized by UNICEF, was held, and was attended by heads of state from 71 countries. At this summit, a World Declaration and Action

子どもの生存、保護、発育に関する「世界宣言」および「行動計画」が採択されました。

　子どもの人権に関して、近年問題となっているのが児童の性的搾取・虐待です。「児童の権利に関する条約」は、当然ながら、このような性的搾取からの児童の保護を定めています。しかし実際には、先進諸国の成人による、途上国、特にアジア地域での児童買春の急増、児童ポルノの氾濫、途上国の児童売買の増加等があります。

　このような背景を踏まえ、1996年にストックホルムにおいて「児童の商業的性的搾取に反対する世界会議」が開催されました。同会議は、スウェーデン政府がユニセフや、NGOとの協力の下で開催したもので、122ヵ国、約20の国際機関、多数のNGOが参加し、「宣言」および「行動のための課題」を採択しました。

　日本においても、児童ポルノや日本人による東南アジアでの児童買春が問題となっており、政府は各省庁連絡会議を開き児童の商業的性的搾取という問題に対する社会全体の認識を高めるための措置について検討しました。

Plan were adopted concerning children's survival, protection, and development.

As for the human rights of children, an issue that in recent years is receiving much attention is the sexual exploitation and abuse of children. The Convention on the Rights of the Child rightly calls for the protection of children from such sexual exploitation. However, at present, there are increasing cases of child prostitution in the developing countries (particularly in the Asian region) involving adults from the developed countries as well as a proliferation of child pornography and an increase of trafficking in children.

Given this situation, the World Congress against Commercial Sexual Exploitation of Children was held in Stockholm in 1996. This Congress, sponsored by the Swedish government in cooperation with UNICEF and NGOs, was attended by representatives from 122 countries, approximately 20 intergovernmental organizations, and many NGOs. It adopted a Declaration and Agenda for Action.

In Japan also, child pornography and child prostitution by Japanese visiting Southeast Asian countries are an issue. The government has held liaison meetings of ministries and agencies concerned to consider measures to increase the awareness of society as a whole about the commercial sexual exploitation of children.

人物紹介

バングラデシュの子供と女性の福利のために働く

**UNICEF
バングラデシュ
広報官**
（くぬぎ じゅんこ）
功刀純子

Kunugi
Junko
**UNICEF
Information/
Communication
Officer**

バングラデシュは1971年に独立しましたが、その後、軍のクーデターが続き、国は大混乱となりました。総選挙が実現して、民政に移行することができたのは、やっと1991年になってからのことでした。バングラデシュの経済の基盤は農業ですが、何年も続いた政情不安のために、食糧を自給する体制は整わず、国民は飢餓に苦しめられてきました。今、貧困の緩和のために、食糧増産、インフレ抑制、農村開発などの計画が進められています。

その暑く、雨ばかりという厳しい気候の国で頑張っている1人の日本女性がいます。ユニセフのバングラデシュ事務所で働く功刀純子さんがその人です。

功刀さんの今の生き方に大きな影響を与えたのは、お父さんの功刀達朗（くぬぎ たつろう）さんでした。お父さんは、長年、国連で活躍してきました。1984年に国連事務次長補に任命され、また、国連国境救援機関(UNBRO)で、カンボジアの難民救済活動に従事したりしています。また、彼女の叔父さんは新聞記者で、功刀さんはそういうお父さん、叔父さんの国際的な活動の姿を見て成長したのです。

アメリカの大学院で彼女はジャーナリズムを専攻しました。在学中、日本の新聞のために、1990年に行われた「世界子供サミット」の記事を書き、そのサミットの取材を通して、子供や女性の権利のために世界

Working for the Welfare of Women and Children in Bangladesh

Bangladesh became an independent state in 1971, but this independence was followed by a military coup d'état and a long period of disorder. It was only in 1991 that general elections successfully brought a transition to civilian government. The Bangladeshi economy is based on agriculture, but because of the long years of political instability, it was difficult to achieve food self-sufficiency and many of the country's people went hungry. Today, various programs are being carried out to reduce poverty, including policies to increase food production, control inflation, and modernize farm villages.

Hard at work in this country of harsh climatic conditions of extreme heat and torrential rains is a Japanese woman named Kunugi Junko. She works for the Bangladesh office of the United Nations Children's Fund (UNICEF).

A great influence on Ms. Kunugi's life is her father, Kunugi Tatsurō, who for many years was active in the United Nations. In 1984 he was appointed a UN Assistant Secretary-General, and with the United Nations Border Relief Organization (UNBRO) he took part in activities to assist refugees from Cambodia. Ms. Kunugi's uncle was a newspaper correspondent. While she was growing up she was always greatly interested in the international activities of both her father and her uncle.

Ms. Kunugi specialized in journalism in graduate school at an American university. While she was in school she wrote articles on the 1990 World Summit for Children for Japanese newspapers. In the process of collecting material about this summit she developed a strong interest in the activities of

人物
紹介

で活躍するユニセフの活動に、強い興味を
抱くようにもなっていました。
　そして1991年、大学院を終えた彼女は、
幸運にも、ユニセフの仕事に就きました。
お父さんの仕事のためにアメリカ、イスラ
エル、スイス、タイなどに移り住み、英語を
母国語のように使いこなしており、そんな彼
女には、ユニセフはぴったりの活躍の場だと
言えます。
　1993年までニューヨークの事務所に勤務
した後、日本政府によるアソシエート・エ
クスパートに選ばれ、ユニセフのベトナム
事務所に広報官補として派遣されました。
そして1996年、功刀さんはバングラデシュ
に来ることになったのです。
　功刀さんの毎日は多忙です。バングラデ
シュの政府といっしょになって、子供の生
活と安全を守り、女性の地位を高めるため
には何が大事かを、広く訴えていかなけれ
ばなりません。衛生上の知識を普及させて
病気・疫病を防ぎ、家族計画の重要性を説
いて人口の増加に歯止めをかけ、貧困のた
めに学校に行っていない子供たちの親に学
校教育の必要性を説き、また、女性の地位
の向上のためには女性が教育を受けること
がいかに大事であるか訴えるなど、様々な
問題の打開のためにユニセフのスタッフと
して精力的な活動が続いています。

**Ms. Kunugi talking with
a Bangladeshi girl.**
(Photo: UNICEF/Shehzad Nocrani)

UNICEF, which is active throughout the world in the interest of women's and children's rights.

In 1991, when she finished her graduate work at the university, she fortunately got a job with UNICEF. Because of her father's work, she had lived in a number of different countries, including the United States, Israel, Switzerland and Thailand, and speaks English as if it were her native language. UNICEF is a workplace that exactly suits her.

After working at the UNICEF headquarters in New York until 1993, Ms. Kunugi was chosen by the Japanese government as an "Associate Expert" and assigned to work as Assistant Information/Communication Officer with the UNICEF office in Viet Nam. In 1996 she came to work with UNICEF in Bangladesh.

Ms. Kunugi is very busy every day. Together with the Government of Bangladesh, she must make known as widely as possible what is needed to protect the lives and well-being of children and to raise the position of women. The UNICEF staff are working energetically to address various types of problems. For example, they strive to prevent epidemics and other illnesses by spreading knowledge about hygiene, to slow population increases by explaining the importance of family planning, and to explain the importance of school education to the parents of children who are not going to school because they are too poor. They also emphasize how important it is for women to get an education in order for them to raise their social and economic position.

世界のために
働くには
To Work
for the World

Chapter

Q 国際的に貢献をしたいのですが、どんな道がありますか？

　　一口に「国際貢献」といっても、国連や
日本政府が、あるいは民間団体が、そして個
人が、それぞれの目的をもって国際協力活動
をしており、活動の内容は多彩です。個々の
詳しい内容は後で説明することにして、主な
活動を概観してみましょう。
　　国連には、まず、国連開発計画(UNDP)と
その実施機関のプロジェクトに基づいて派遣
されるフィールド専門家という制度がありま
す。経験の豊かな専門家がいろいろな分野で
開発途上国に派遣され、その発展に寄与し
ています。このフィールド専門家への日本人

Japan Overseas Cooperation Volunteers helping with efforts to rebuild Cambodia's economy and society display a poster they have helped make in order to advertise Cambodia as a tourist destination.

Q I'd like to contribute internationally, but how can I do this?

The term "international contributions" covers a great variety of cooperative activities, with many different purposes, undertaken by the United Nations, the Japanese government, and nongovernmental groups and individuals. Leaving more detailed descriptions for later, let's take an overview of some of the main activities.

Within the United Nations organization, there is a system for sending Field Experts on the basis of the needs of the United Nations Development Program (UNDP) and the projects of bodies that carry out work under its guidance. Experts with ample experience in various fields are sent to developing countries to contribute to these countries' growth and pros-

の進出はまだまだ少ないのが現状です。

　さらに国連には、国連ボランティア(UNV)という機関があります。1993年、選挙監視員としてカンボジアに派遣されていた中田厚仁さんが凶弾に倒れるという悲劇がありましたが、中田さんはこの国連ボランティアとして活動していました。UNVの活動は140以上の分野にわたっています。
　また日本政府は国際協力活動の1つとして開発途上国に技術協力の専門家を派遣しています。この業務は国際協力事業団(JICA)が行っており、これまでにいろいろな分野で、約4万人の専門家が開発途上国に派遣されています。

　以上のような経験豊かな専門家の活動も大事ですが、若い人たちにとっては、青年海外協力隊の隊員になって、開発途上国で汗を流してくるという道もあります。これは1965年から開始された政府の事業で、国際協力事業団の中に事務局があります。
　また、外務省では、将来、国連などで働く正規の国際公務員を志望する青年のために、一定期間、いろいろな国際機関に勤務して専門知識を深め、経験を積むアソシエート・エキスパート制度を作っています。

　こういった国連や政府が行っている活動のほかに、財団法人海外貿易開発協会などが民間レベルで専門家を開発途上国に派遣していますし、近年特に注目されるのがNGOのグループの活動です。NGOの活動は実に多彩で、国際貢献は人それぞれが可

perity. The number of Japanese who have applied to work in these Field Expert positions is still relatively small.

Within the United Nations organization, there is a body with the name United Nations Volunteers (UNV). Nakata Atsuhito, who was tragically killed by a bullet in Cambodia in 1993, had been working as a United Nations Volunteer sent to Cambodia to monitor elections there. The work of United Nations Volunteers embraces over 140 categories of activities.

Another category of international cooperation efforts carried out by the Japanese government is the dispatch of experts for technical cooperation to developing countries. This work is administered by the Japan International Cooperation Agency (JICA), which has up to now sent approximately 40,000 experts to developing countries to work in many different fields.

Besides the above-mentioned types of activities by experts with ample experience, younger people have opportunities for working in developing countries as members of the Japan Overseas Cooperation Volunteers (JOCV). These government-sponsored activities began in 1965 and their administrative headquarters are within JICA.

The Ministry of Foreign Affairs has an Associate Expert Program through which young persons interested in becoming full-time international civil servants working with the United Nations, etc., can, for limited periods of time, work in various international organizations, thus gaining valuable experience and deepening specialized know-how.

Besides these activities carried out by the United Nations and by the Japanese government, experts are sent to developing countries on a nongovernmental level by groups such as the Overseas Trade Development Association (OTDA). Such activities by NGO groups have attracted much attention in recent years. The activities of NGOs are

能な形で参加することができるものと考える
べきです。

Q 国連や政府で国際協力の専門家になるためにはどんな適性、能力が求められますか。

まず必要なことは「国際性」です。しかし
国際性とはどんなことを言うのでしょうか。

国際協力の専門家は、開発途上国で自分
たちとは異なった国籍の人々と共に仕事を進
めていくわけですから、異なる文化、言語、
宗教、風習などの数々の「異質」な壁を乗
り越えることができるかが、まず試練の1つ
となります。そして単に「乗り越える」だけ
ではなく、その国の文化、歴史に尊敬と信頼
を示して、対等の立場で協力をしていくこと
ができることが必要です。

同時に、自分が専門とする知識・技術を
持っているかどうかが問われます。国内でも
十分に通用する実戦的な専門知識、技術が
備わっていなければならないことは当然で
す。そのためには、日本での実務経験がある
ことも大事な条件の1つになります。

そういうプロとしての知識・技術を備えた
上で、さらに創造的な精神、チャレンジング
な姿勢があるかどうかも大事です。また、組
織の中で活動をしていく能力も必要です。

最後にもう1つ大事なことは語学です。特
に英語をマスターしておくことが必要ですし、
ほかに国連の公用語であるフランス語、中国
語、スペイン語、ロシア語、アラビア語のど

truly multifaceted and individuals can participate internationally in the ways they can handle best.

Q To become an international cooperation expert for the United Nations or for the Japanese government, what sorts of aptitudes and abilities are required?

What is required, first of all, is "international sensibility." What, however, is meant by this expression?

Because international cooperation experts must carry out their work in developing countries with people of nationalities different from their own, the foremost challenge is whether they are able to overcome the barriers of various sorts of "differentness" with respect to culture, language, religion, manners, etc. It's not just a matter of "overcoming," but of being able to show respect for, and display trust in another country's culture and history, and to be able to work together on a basis of equality.

Whether or not the applicant has some specialized knowledge and skills will also come into question. It is only reasonable to expect that the applicant should have specialized knowledge and skills of a practical nature that could also be applied at home. Having had practical experience in Japan is one important condition.

In addition to professional knowledge and skills, it is also important to know whether the applicant has a creative spirit and an outlook that welcomes new challenges. Also, he or she should be able to work in an organizational setting.

Finally, another important factor is language ability. It is necessary, in particular, to have a good working knowledge of English, and it would be an asset to have some ability in one of the other official languages of the United Nations (i.e.,

れか1つぐらいはマスターしたほうが有利です。同時に派遣された現地の言葉をマスターしていく積極性がなければ、なかなか現地に溶け込むことはできないかも知れません。

 国連のフィールド専門家とは?
応募するにはどうすればいいですか。

　　国連の目的は、国連憲章の中で次のように定められています。
(1) 国際の平和と安全を維持すること
(2) 諸国間の友好関係を発展させること
(3) 経済的、社会的、文化的、または人道的問題を解決し、人権、および基本的自由の尊重をはかるために国際協力を行うこと

　　この憲章の下に、国連の組織下にある国際機関は、各国政府からの要請があった場合、それにこたえて、必要とされる分野の専門家を派遣しています。この専門家をフィールド専門家と呼んでいます。
　　派遣された国の政府、または公的な機関に対するアドバイザーとして働きますので、専門分野について相当の知識、経験が必要とされます。

応募するには——
　　援助受け入れ国の要請によってプロジェクトが決まり、その内容に応じた専門家ポストの職務明細書が作成されていますから、それを見て応募します。
　　資格には制限はありませんが、応募者はあくまで、要請国が求める分野ですでに十分な

French, Chinese, Spanish, Russian, or Arabic). It is likely to be difficult to fit in well with the local society unless the applicant also shows an active willingness to master the local language of the place to which he or she is sent.

Q What is a UN Field Expert? How does one apply for this job?

The purposes of the United Nations are set out in the UN Charter as follows:
(1) to maintain international peace and security;
(2) to develop friendly relations among nations;
(3) to achieve international cooperation in solving international problems of an economic, social, cultural, or humanitarian character and in promoting and encouraging respect for human rights and fundamental freedoms.

In response to requests from the governments of various countries, international bodies within the United Nations organization, under the UN Charter, send to these countries experts in fields where they are seen as needed. The United Nations organization calls these persons Field Experts.

These Field Experts work as advisors to the central governments or to other public bodies in the countries to which they are sent, and so they need to have considerable knowledge and experience in their specialized fields.

To apply—

Projects are decided upon according to requests from the countries receiving assistance. Detailed written descriptions of the expert posts available for each project are drawn up for prospective applicants to study before making their applications.

There are no formal limitations in regard to eligibility to apply, but it must be understood as necessary that appli-

専門家であることが前提となります。

応募用紙には、自分が応募したポストに対する自分の専門や適性を十分に証明できるように、具体的な事実を挙げて記入します。

採用は派遣国際機関および受け入れ国の選考によって決まります。

問い合わせ先——
外務省国際社会協力部　国連行政課
国際機関人事センター
住所：〒100-8919
東京都千代田区霞が関 2-2-1
電話：03-3580-3311　内線2840-1

Q 国連ボランティアとは?
応募するにはどうすればいいですか。

フィールド専門家の派遣に加え、国連開発計画(UNDP)の機構内に作られているのが国連ボランティア(UNV)計画で、この機関が派遣しているのが国連ボランティアです。

国連ボランティアとして開発途上国に派遣される専門家の多くは、専門分野における高度な知識と長い職務経験を有しており、その派遣の分野は、140以上の広範囲にわたっています。

登録制度となっていて、受け入れ機関や政府等からUNVに対して正式の要請があり、登録されたリストの中から該当する人が選定されていく仕組みになっています。

cants must be sufficiently specialized in the fields for which the requesting countries are seeking their help.

On the application form, the applicant gives specific factual information to establish his or her specialty and suitability for the post to which he or she has applied.

Acceptance for a post is decided upon through a selection process that involves both the international body and the recipient country.

Contact address for further information—

Recruitment Center for International Organizations
United Nations Administration Division
Department of Multilateral Cooperation
Ministry of Foreign Affairs
Address: Kasumigaseki 2–2–1, Chiyoda-ku, Tokyo 100–8919
Phone: 03–3580–3311, extensions 2840/1

Q What is a United Nations Volunteer?
And how should I apply for the job?

In addition to the program for sending Field Experts, there is the United Nations Volunteers (UNV) Program administered as part of the United Nations Development Program (UNDP).

The specialists who are working in developing countries as United Nations Volunteers have high levels of knowledge and long career experience in a specific area. There are over 140 fields in which these specialists have been sent to work.

There is a registration system by which the international bodies and national governments who wish to receive these experts first make formal requests to the UNV Program. After that, appropriate personnel are selected from lists of

応募するには——

　開発途上国が必要とする技術や技能を持っている人であればだれでも応募する資格があります。年齢も特に制限はありません。青年海外協力隊事務局も人材の確保に協力しており、そのOB隊員も登録されています。その他の経験を持つ人はUNDP東京事務所および外務省国際ボランティア登録センターが窓口となっています。

問い合わせ先——

国連開発計画(UNDP)東京連絡事務所
住所：〒150-0001
東京都渋谷区神宮前 5-53-70 国連大学ビル
電話：03-5467-4751

外務省国際社会協力部　国連行政課
国際機関人事センター内
国際ボランティア登録センター
住所：〒100-8919
東京都千代田区霞が関 2-2-1
電話：03-3580-3311 内線 2819

国際協力事業団・青年海外協力隊事務局
住所：〒151-0053
東京都渋谷区代々木 2-1-1
新宿マインズタワー 6階
電話：03-5352-7261

persons who have registered and are available.

To apply—

Anyone is eligible to apply so long as he or she has technical knowledge or other skills needed in developing countries. There is no formal age limitation. The office of the Japan Overseas Cooperation Volunteers (JOCV) cooperates in finding participants from Japan, and many former JOCV volunteers are registered as available for UNV activities. Persons without JOCV experience, but having other experience making them suitable for UNV work, may apply through the UNDP Tokyo Office or the UN Volunteers Registration Center in the Ministry of Foreign Affairs.

Contact addresses for further information—

UNDP Tokyo Office
United Nations University Building
Address: Jingūmae 5–53–70, Shibuya-ku, Tokyo 150–0001
Phone: 03–5467–4751

UN Volunteers Registration Center
c/o Recruitment Center for International Organizations
United Nations Administration Division, Department of
Multilateral Cooperation, Ministry of Foreign Affairs
Address: Kasumigaseki 2–2–1, Chiyoda-ku, Tokyo 100–8919
Phone: 03–3580–3311, extension 2819

Japan Overseas Cooperation Volunteers Head Office
c/o Japan International Cooperation Agency
Address: Shinjuku Maynds Tower, 6th Floor
Yoyogi 2–1–1, Shibuya-ku, Tokyo 151–0053
Phone: 03–5352–7261

Q 国連のアソシエート・エキスパートとは? 応募するにはどうすればいいですか。

　外務省では、将来、正規の国際公務員を志望する若い日本人のために、アソシエート・エキスパート制度を設けています。一定期間、各国際機関で職員として勤務することにより、専門知識を深め国際的業務の体験を積む実地研修の機会を提供することが目的で、その中から正規の職員として採用される人たちが出てきています。正規の職員になるための1つのステップです。

応募するには——

　受験年の4月1日現在32歳以下の日本国籍の方であればだれでも応募できます。ただし、大学卒業後、自分が専攻した分野またはその類似分野で2年以上の実務の経験があること、または大学院を修了した人という制限があります。

　語学については、英語あるいはフランス語のいずれかで仕事を遂行するだけの力があることが必要です。

問い合わせ先——

外務省国際社会協力部　国連行政課
国際機関人事センター
住所：〒100-8919
東京都千代田区霞が関 2-2-1
電話：03-3580-3311　内線 2840-1

Q What is a UN Associate Expert? And how should I apply for this job?

The Ministry of Foreign Affairs has an Associate Expert Program for young Japanese who are interested in becoming regular staff members of international bodies in the future. Its purpose is to provide opportunities to deepen specialized know-how and to build up experience with international work projects through working as staff members of these international organizations for certain periods. Some of these Associate Experts may later be selected to work as official field experts. Experience as an Associate Expert can be a step toward becoming a regular staff member of an international body.

To apply—

Any person of Japanese nationality who is no more than 32 years old on the date of the application exam (April 1) may apply. Moreover, after graduation from a university, an applicant must have had more than 2 years of practical experience in the field he or she specialized in or in a related field, or alternatively, must have completed a program of graduate studies.

As for language competence, it is necessary to be able to carry out work assignments in either English or French.

Contact address for further information—

Recruitment Center for International Organizations
United Nations Administration Division
Department of Multilateral Cooperation
Ministry of Foreign Affairs
Address: Kasumigaseki 2–2–1, Chiyoda-ku, Tokyo 100–8919
Phone: 03–3580–3311, extensions 2840/1

Q アジア生産性機構(APO)とは? その専門家として 活動するにはどうすればいいですか?

1961年に設立された国際機関で、アジアの国々の経済の発展、人々の生活水準の向上のためには、経済活動の生産性の向上が欠かせないという観点で作られたものです。アジアの18の国と地域が加盟しています。

その活動の1つが専門家の派遣です。TES(技術専門家派遣サービス)という制度に基づいて行われています。加盟国の要請に基づいて派遣された専門家は、経営や技術の診断や指導、生産性向上のための提言などを行います。

応募するには——

年齢や性別は問いませんが、特定の分野において専門的な十分な知識と、ある期間の実務経験を持っていることが必要です。

それに英語の力が必要です。この仕事には通訳はつかないことが通例になっています。

問い合わせ先——

アジア生産性機構
住所: 〒107-0052
東京都港区赤坂 8-4-14
電話: 03-3408-7221

Q What is the Asian Productivity Organization (APO)? How does one become one of its Technical Experts?

The APO is an intergovernmental regional organization established in 1961 with the view that for the sake of developing the economies and raising people's living standards in Asian countries, it would be indispensable to raise the productivity of economic endeavors. Eighteen countries/regions of Asia and the Pacific are presently members.

One of its activities is to send experts to its member countries. This is done through its Technical Expert Services (TES) program. Experts who are sent upon requests from the member countries make diagnoses of relevant problems, either managerial or technological, and make necessary recommendations to improve productivity.

How to Register as an APO Expert—

Neither age nor gender is an issue, but it is necessary to have specialized knowledge and a certain period of practical experience in some specific field. A good command of spoken and written English is essential. In most cases, no interpreting services are available during the work to be undertaken.

Contact address for further information—

Asian Productivity Organization
Address: Akasaka 8–4–14, Minato-ku, Tokyo 107–0052
Phone: 03–3408–7221

国際協力事業団(JICA)による
政府ベースの技術協力専門家とは?
それに応募するには
どうすればいいですか。

　　国際協力事業団は、1974年に、それまで
の海外技術協力事業や海外移住事業を引き
継いで新しく設立された特殊法人です。

　　その主な仕事には、政府ベースの技術協力
事業、技術協力のための人材の確保・養成、
開発協力事業、そして「青年海外協力隊」
の派遣事業などがあります。

　　技術協力のための専門家は、各国、ある
いは国際機関からの要請に応じて適宜派遣
され、これまでに約4万人を超える人たちが
派遣されています。

応募するには——
　　原則として大学卒業程度の学歴で、年齢
は30歳以上、60歳未満です。それぞれの分
野において、技術協力に従事するのに十分な
専門技術を持っていることが必要です。
　　春と秋の年2回専門家の公募を行っている
ほか、専門家希望者をあらかじめ登録し、各
国からの要請に基づいて選ばれる登録制度が
あります。

問い合わせ先——
国際協力事業団　国際協力総合研修所
住所：〒162–0845
東京都新宿区市ヶ谷本村町10–5
電話：03–3269–3201

Q What about government-sponsored technical cooperation experts sent through the Japan International Cooperation Agency? How can I apply?

The Japan International Cooperation Agency (JICA) is a special-status public corporation established in 1974 to take over the management of already-existing activities in the fields of emigration and overseas technical cooperation.

Its major activities today are intergovernmental technical cooperation, the recruitment and training of personnel for technical cooperation projects, development assistance, and the sending abroad of Japan Overseas Cooperation Volunteers (JOCV).

Over 40,000 technical cooperation experts have been dispatched abroad under JICA sponsorship at the requests of various countries and international bodies.

To apply—

As a general rule, applicants should be university graduates between the ages of 30 and 60. They must have adequate expertise in the fields in which they intend to do technical cooperation work.

Recruitment of experts is carried out twice a year, in spring and in autumn, and specialists are also registered in advance and then selected to be sent abroad in accordance with requests from recipient countries

Contact address for further information—

Institute for International Cooperation
Japan International Cooperation Agency
Address: Ichigaya Honmura-chō 10–5, Shinjuku-ku, Tokyo 162–0845

Q 青年海外協力隊とは? 隊員になるには どうすればいいですか?

「青年海外協力隊」は国際協力事業団の活動の主要なものの1つで、青年海外協力隊事務局(JOCV)がその業務を担当しています。

青年海外協力隊事業は、「開発途上地域の住民と一体となって当該地域の経済及び社会の発展に協力することを目的とする海外での青年の活動を促進し、及び助長する」事業です。協力隊員は、開発途上国の要請に基づいて派遣されます。

協力隊員の活動の基本姿勢は、「現地の人々と共に」という言葉に集約されています。隊員たちは派遣された国の人々と共に生活し、働き、彼らの言葉を話し、相互理解を図りながら、彼らの自助努力を促進させる形で協力活動を展開しています。

派遣を受け入れた国と日本との間の国際的な取り決めに基づき、1997年までに約1万7000人の隊員が派遣されており、そのうち30%は女性です。

協力隊員の活動内容は多種多様で、農業土木、陶芸、工芸、医療、看護、スポーツの指導など150以上の職種に分かれています。派遣国は世界に広がりますが、やはり人数が多いのはアジア、アフリカの諸国です。

こうした協力隊の活動は、内外から高く評

Phone: 03–3269–3201

Q What about the Japan Overseas Cooperation Volunteers? How can I become a member?

The Japan Overseas Cooperation Volunteers (JOCV) is administered by the JOCV secretariat within the Japan International Cooperation Agency (JICA) and constitutes a major branch of JICA activities.

The objective of JOCV is "to promote and assist the overseas activities of youths whose purpose is to cooperate, in unity with the people of developing areas, in the economic and social development of those areas." The JOCV volunteers are sent on assignments on the basis of specific requests from each developing country.

The basic policy underlying JOCV activities is summarized in the phrase "with local people." The JOCV members develop cooperation activities by promoting self-help efforts together with people in the countries to which they are sent by living and working with them, speaking their languages, and keeping mutual understanding always in mind.

Through 1997, there have been approximately 17,000 JOCV members, of which about 30 percent are women, under international agreements concluded between Japan and the countries to which these voluteers are sent.

JOCV activities are of many types, divided into over 150 categories, including agricultural civil engineering, pottery and handicrafts, medicine, nursing, and sports training, to mention just a few. JOCV members are sent to countries all over the world, though particularly large numbers are found working in Asian and African countries.

Such activities are highly valued both at home and

価されており、相手国からの派遣要請も年々
増加しています。

問い合わせ先——
国際協力事業団
青年海外協力隊事務局
住所：〒151-0053
東京都渋谷区代々木 2-1-1
新宿マインズタワー 6 階
電話：03-5352-7261

Q 財団法人海外貿易開発協会(JODC)が
派遣する民間専門家とは?
応募するには
どうすればいいですか。

　　これまでの国連や政府による専門家の派遣
に加えて、民間レベルでも開発途上国に専門
家を派遣している組織があります。その代表
的なものがこの海外貿易開発協会です。

　　海外貿易開発協会は、開発途上地域での
産業の開発の促進、途上国と日本の貿易の
振興、途上国に対する技術協力の促進を目
的としています。そしてそのために、民間専
門家の派遣業務をしています。

応募するには——
　　専門分野において指導できる技術的知識、
経験を持っていることが必要です。また、職
務の推進に必要な英語力も必要です。

abroad. At the same time, requests from developing countries are increasing year by year.

Contact address for further information—
Japan Overseas Cooperation Volunteers Head Office
c/o Japan International Cooperation Agency
Address: Shinjuku Maynds Tower, 6th Floor
Yoyogi 2–1–1, Shibuya-ku, Tokyo 151–0053
Phone: 03–5352–7261

Q What about the private-sector experts sent abroad by the Japan Overseas Development Corporation? How can one apply?

Besides what we have discussed so far, namely, the sending of experts abroad by the United Nations and by the Japanese government, we should also mention organizations at the nongovernmental level that send experts to developing countries. An important example is the Japan Overseas Development Corporation (JODC).

The purpose of this organization is to support the development of industries in developing regions, to stimulate trade between developing countries and Japan, and to promote technical cooperation with developing countries. To this end, it carries out a program to send experts abroad at the nongovernmental level.

To apply —
It is necessary to have technical knowledge and experience in the specialized field in which guidance is to be offered. Another requirement is adequate English language

　応募の資格は25歳から65歳までですから、日本の会社での定年を終えた人たちにも十分に機会があります。また、日本在住10年以上の外国人にも応募資格があります。

問い合わせ先――
財団法人海外貿易開発協会　派遣事業部
住所：〒107-0001
東京都港区虎ノ門4-3-13　秀和神谷町ビル
電話：03-5473-0980

Q NGOって何ですか。

　NGOとは、Non-Governmental Organizationの略語で、「非政府組織」または「民間団体」と呼ばれます。これはたとえば国連憲章の第71条の中でも使われている用語で、国連、政府、官公庁が設立した団体や機関、また営利を目的とした企業による組織などとは区別して用いています。現在では一般的に、ボランティアとして海外協力を行っている市民の組織をNGOと呼んでいます。

　日本でこのような市民組織が生まれてきたのは1960年代に入ってからで、特に1970年末にタイの国境沿いに大量に流出したインドシナ難民の支援をきっかけに、多くのNGOが誕生しました。
　1995年の阪神・淡路大震災で多数のボランティアが被災者の支援に駆けつけました

ability for undertaking the assigned work.

Because the age of applicants can be from 25 to 65, these activities offer many opportunities to persons who have retired from Japanese companies. Foreigners who have lived in Japan for ten or more years can also apply.

Contact address for further information—
Overseas Dispatch Department
Japan Overseas Development Corporation
Address: Shūwa Kamiya-chō Building
Toranomon 4–3–13, Minato-ku, Tokyo 107–0001
Phone: 03–5473–0980

Q What are NGOs?

NGO is an abbreviation for "nongovernmental organization," corresponding to *hiseifu soshiki* or *minkan dantai* (literally "group composed of private citizens") in Japanese. The term NGO is used, for example, in Article 71 of the United Nations Charter, which distinguishes such organizations from organizations set up by the UN, national governments and other official bodies, as well as from organizations set up by private companies for the purpose of monetary profit. Today, citizens' organizations which volunteer cooperative efforts in other countries are generally referred to as "NGOs."

In Japan, these citizens' organizations came into being in the early 1960s. Especially toward the end of the 1970s, many NGOs were formed to offer assistance to Indochinese refugees who had fled in large numbers across border areas into Thailand.

Many volunteers quickly came to the assistance of victims of the Hanshin-Awaji Earthquake in 1995, and follow-

が、それを機会に日本でもボランティアについての意識がさらに高まり、NGOの活動は年々活発になってきていると言われます。

その活動の内容も多彩で、対象の地域もこれまでのアジア、アフリカ中心から、中南米、ロシアへも広がっているほか、国内で在日外国人のための支援活動などを行う組織も増えつつあります。その数は正確にはわかっていません。全体で約3000ぐらいあるのではないかとも言われ、その内、直接海外援助活動を行うNGOは約350ぐらいと言われています。

NGOの資金源は多くの場合、個人や団体からの会費や寄付金、国からの助成金が主なものになります。またボランティアにかかわる国の産物などを販売して資金を得ている場合もあります。

Q NGOは国際ボランティアとしてどのような活動をしていますか。

NGOの団体の活動の仕方は団体によって様々ですが、おおよそ次のような活動内容に分けることができます。
①人材の派遣による支援
教育、農業、医療、地域産業の振興などの様々な分野、あるいは災害復旧などに、短期あるいは長期に人材を派遣して協力をするものです。

②カウンターパート支援
カウンターパート(counterpart)とは「対応するもの」という意味で、現地に人材を派

ing this tragedy, awareness of volunteer work has grown in Japan where it is often remarked that NGO activities become more prominent with each passing year.

The international activities of Japanese NGOs are quite varied and, while geographically concentrated in Asia and Africa, extend also to regions such as Central and South America, and Russia. A growing number of organizations are also engaged in activities to help foreigners living in Japan. The exact number of Japanese NGOs is not known but it is thought to be approximately 3,000. Among them, approximately 350 are NGOs that carry out activities of direct assistance to people in other countries.

In many cases, the main source of NGO funds are dues and donations from individuals and groups, together with subsidies from the Japanese government. There are also cases where funds are gathered through the sale of products from countries where volunteer activities are carried out.

Q What sorts of activities do NGOs, as international volunteers, engage in?

The ways in which NGO activities are carried out depend on the organization in question, but in general the types of activities can be put into the following six categories:

(1) Assistance through the sending of volunteers from Japan

These NGOs provide assistance by sending personnel over short or longer periods to help in a variety of fields such as education, agriculture, medical treatment, and the promotion of industries in rural areas, and also to help with rehabilitation work in the wake of disasters.

(2) Counterpart assistance

The word *counterpart* means something that corresponds to, or exists in response to, something else. Counterpart assis-

遣するのではなく、対応する現地のNGOや福祉団体に、資金を提供したり、物資の供給をしたりして支援するものです。

③国内研修による支援

特に開発途上国の人たちを日本に招いて、各種の技術を身につけてもらうための講座や、実習の場を提供する活動をしています。研修を受けた人たちは故国に帰って、それぞれの分野の専門家として活躍していきます。

④在日・滞日外国人に対する支援

日本に滞在する人たちの事情は様々です。その滞在の事情の是非はともかくとして、中には日本で不利な生活を強いられている外国人がたくさんいます。そのような外国人に対して、教育、医療、福祉などのサービスを提供するものです。

⑤フェアトレードによる支援

現地で作られた手工芸品、織物、食品などを公正な価格で買い上げ、現地の生産者の生活の向上をはかるための支援です。日本側の購買者はそういう製品を通じて現地の文化や生活を学ぶことができるという利点があります。

⑥情報の提供、問題の提起

貧困、人権侵害、環境破壊など、世界各地で起こっている問題についての情報を集めて提供し、さらに問題提起をする活動です。

tance is basically not the sending of people from Japan to other countries but help in the form of providing materials and funds for the use of related NGOs and welfare organizations abroad.

(3) Assistance for training in Japan

These NGOs invite persons from abroad (especially from developing countries) to come to Japan to familiarize themselves with various types of work and skills, and they arrange lectures and provide training facilities for these purposes. Those who have had such training in Japan very often become active as experts in diverse fields upon their return to their home countries.

(4) Assistance to foreigners living in Japan

The circumstances of people from abroad living in Japan are varied. And while not going into all the details of their stays, it is true that many of them are living in Japan under unfavorable circumstances. There are a number of NGOs which offer such people services in the fields of education, medical care, or in other areas that contribute to their welfare.

(5) Help through "fair trade"

This sort of assistance helps to improve the lives of producers in other countries by organizing the sale in Japan, at fair prices, of food products, textiles, handicrafts, etc., produced in these countries.

(6) Providing information and raising public issues

These NGOs collect and make available information on various types of problems around the world, including poverty, violations of human rights, and environmental degradation. They are also active in raising these issues in forums for public discussion.

Q 国際ボランティア活動には どのような参加の方法がありますか。

　参加の方法には大きく分けて次のようなパターンがあります。

①ワークキャンプによる参加型

　一定の期間、通常は2〜3週間ほど、特定のプロジェクトの一員として加わって共同生活をして活動します。活動の分野は様々ですが、植林、環境の保存、考古学の調査、農作業、建物の建設・修復などが多いようです。

②長期滞在による参加型

　1年、あるいはそれ以上にわたって、現地に滞在して開発活動に従事するものです。プロとしてそれなりの知識や経験を生かして活動することが多く、多くの場合、現地での生活費、渡航費が支給されます。

　長期ですから、自分の仕事を止めたり、休職したりして参加することになりますが、最近では日本でも、長期のボランティア休暇を認める会社も出てきていますから、これからは長期の参加が可能になる人たちが増えてくるでしょう。

③通勤による参加型

　ボランティアとして働く場所に通って活動します。フルタイムの場合もあれば、特定の日だけのパートタイムの場合もあり、活動団体と話し合って都合のつく時間を活用していきます。通例、自分が住むところは自分で探し、自活していかねばなりませんから、現地

Q What sorts of ways are there to participate in international volunteer activities?

Ways of participating, roughly categorized, include the following:

(1) Participating in work camps

In this type of activity, one becomes a member of a certain project for a limited period of time (typically around 2 or 3 weeks), working and living together with other project members during this time. There are many possible fields of activity, including planting trees, protecting the environment, archaeological surveys, agricultural projects and the construction or renovation of buildings.

(2) Long-term residence

In this type of activity, a participant engages in development-related work while living abroad for a year or more. In many cases this involves making use of one's knowledge and experience as a professional in a certain field. Living expenses abroad and the expenses of travel to and from the host country are usually provided by the sponsoring organization.

Because such residence is for a long period, in order to participate in such projects the participant must either quit his or her present work in Japan or arrange for a leave of absence. Recently in Japan some companies have shown flexibility in giving their employees such leaves of absence to take part in long-term volunteer work, and so the number of participants in such activities will surely grow.

(3) Participation that involves commuting from one's home

In this pattern, the participant commutes to the place where he or she works as a volunteer. This may include full-time work but there are also cases of volunteering on a part-time basis, for example, on just certain days or during certain hours that will be agreed upon in consultation with the volunteer group. In most of these cases, the volunteer selects his

への留学、ホームステイのかたわらというケースが多いようです。

④緊急参加型

1995年の阪神・淡路大震災や、1997年の日本海の重油流出事故の時のように、人災や天災によって引き起こされた緊急事態の援助の一員として参加するものです。

⑤実習訓練(internship)参加型

アメリカの大学では在学中に非営利団体や企業などで実習生として現場活動の経験を積む制度があり、大学の単位としても認められています。夏休みなどを利用して働き、この経験をもとに就職したり、ボランティア活動に入っていくのです。外国人の学生にもインターンシップの門戸を開いているアメリカその他の団体がたくさんあります。

 Q NGOの国際ボランティア活動について どんなところで情報を 得ることができますか。

国際協力プラザ

国際協力に関する最新の情報を取りそろえたコミュニケーションの場所です。広いフロアには国際協力活動をしている団体の報告書や国内外の雑誌がそろっています。自治体の事業紹介やNGO段階の活動紹介のパンフ

or her own place of residence and is responsible for taking care of the details of daily living. There are many cases where such volunteer work is combined with overseas study or homestays.

(4) Emergency activities

These cases involve participation as a member of aid groups to cope with emergency situations brought about by man-made or natural disasters, such as the Hanshin-Awaji Earthquake in 1995 or the serious oil spill that polluted the coast of the Sea of Japan in early 1997.

(5) Internships

In many American universities, there is a system by which students, during their course of studies, can gain experience in places outside the university (including other countries) as "interns" with companies or nonprofit organizations. Such experience can even be counted as credits toward graduation from the university. In many cases, students engage in these sorts of "internship" volunteer activities during their summer vacations and later make use of these experiences after finding formal employment or in further volunteer activities. There are many organizations in the United States and elsewhere whose doors are open to students from Japan and other countries to take part in these sorts of internships.

Q Where is information available about NGO international volunteer activities?

The International Cooperation Plaza

This is a forum for communication that brings together the most recent information about international cooperation opportunities. Within its large floor space, one can find a full range of reports and journals published in Japan and abroad by organizations engaged in international coop-

レットも整理されています。多数の興味深い
映像資料もそろっています。また、ワークキ
ャンプの案内やNGOボランティア募集の情
報の掲示があります。利用は無料。

住所：122ページ参照

　現在では各地域に活動拠点を置くNGOも
多く、また、都道府県や市町村単位で地域
における国際交流活動を勧めている団体とし
て国際交流協会があります。それぞれが住む
地方自治体の広報課や国際交流課あるいは
国際交流協会に問い合わせてみるのも、身近
な情報を得る方法です。

eration activities. There are many pamphlets introducing the activities of local governments and NGOs. There are also many interesting audiovisual materials and displays that give useful information on work camps and the recruitment of NGO volunteers. Use of the International Cooperation Plaza is free of charge.

Address: See p.122

Today there are many NGOs whose base of activities is outside Tokyo, and there are numerous international exchange associations which promote international exchange activities at the prefectural, city, town, and village level. One way to get close-at-hand information is to consult these international exchange associations or, alternatively, the Public Information Division or International Exchange Division of local governments where you live.

索引
INDEX

日本語索引

さ

し

英語索引

国際貢献Q&A　世界で活躍する日本人
Japan's Contribution to the World

1999年2月19日　第1刷発行

編　者　　外務省大臣官房海外広報課

発行者　　野間佐和子

発行所　　講談社インターナショナル株式会社
　　　　　〒112-8652　東京都文京区音羽1-17-14
　　　　　電話：03-3944-6493（編集）
　　　　　　　　03-3944-6492（営業）

印刷所　　大日本印刷株式会社

製本所　　株式会社 堅省堂

Copyright © 1999 by Ministry of Foreign Affairs of Japan; Overseas
Public Relations Division
ISBN4-7700-2192-5

英語と日本語で楽しむ

対訳 サザエさん (全12巻)

The Wonderful World of Sazae-san

長谷川町子 著　ジュールス・ヤング 訳

- 吹き出しの中にオリジナルの暖かい雰囲気を大切にした英語、コマの横に日本語がつく対訳形式。

- お正月、こいのぼり、忘年会など日本独特の文化や習慣には、欄外に英語の解説つき。

46判変型（113 x 188 mm）仮製

第 1 巻	170ページ	ISBN 4-7700-2075-9
第 2 巻	168ページ	ISBN 4-7700-2093-7
第 3 巻	198ページ	ISBN 4-7700-2094-5
第 4 巻	164ページ	ISBN 4-7700-2149-6
第 5 巻	176ページ	ISBN 4-7700-2150-X
第 6 巻	160ページ	ISBN 4-7700-2151-8
第 7 巻	168ページ	ISBN 4-7700-2152-6
第 8 巻	168ページ	ISBN 4-7700-2153-4
第 9 巻	172ページ	ISBN 4-7700-2154-2
第10巻	172ページ	ISBN 4-7700-2155-0
第11巻	176ページ	ISBN 4-7700-2156-9
第12巻	168ページ	ISBN 4-7700-2157-7
化粧箱入り全12巻セット		ISBN 4-7700-2435-5

対訳 英語で話す日本経済Q&A
A Bilingual Guide to the Japanese Economy

NHK国際放送局経済プロジェクト・
大和総研経済調査部 編
46判（128 x 188 mm）仮製 368ページ
ISBN 4-7700-1942-4

NHK国際放送で好評を得た番組が本になりました。クイズと
会話形式で楽しく読んでいくうちに、日本経済の仕組が分かり、
同時に英語にも強くなっていきます。日本語と英語の対応が
ひと目で分かる編集上の工夫もいっぱい。

対訳 おくのほそ道
The Narrow Road to Oku

松尾芭蕉 著　ドナルド・キーン 訳
宮田雅之 切り絵
A5判変型（140 x 226 mm）
仮製 188ページ（カラー口絵41点）
ISBN 4-7700-2028-7

古典文学の最高峰のひとつ「おくのほそ道」を、ドナルド・
キーンが新訳しました。画家、宮田雅之が精魂を込めた切り絵
の魅力とあいまって、この名作に新しい生命が吹き込まれた、
必読の1冊です。

対訳 竹取物語
The Tale of the Bamboo Cutter

川端康成 現代語訳
ドナルド・キーン 英訳
宮田雅之 切り絵
A5判変型 横長（226 x 148 mm）
仮製 箱入り180ページ（カラー口絵16点）
ISBN 4-7700-2329-4

ノーベル賞作家の現代語訳と傑出した芸術家の作品、そして
日本文学の研究に一生を捧げたジャパノロジストの翻訳が合
体した、大人のための「竹取物語」。

バイリンガル とってもかんたんマイレシピ
Stone Soup : Easy Japanese Home Cooking

渡辺節子 著
B5判変型（189 x 257 mm）仮製 256ページ
ISBN 4-7700-2061-9

手軽な日本の家庭料理、わが家の味160品目の作り方を英語
と日本語で紹介したクッキングブック。作り方や調理器具な
どのイラスト付き、カロリー計算・調理時間もひと目で分か
ります。

対訳 日本事典 (全1巻)

The Kodansha Bilingual Encyclopedia of Japan

講談社インターナショナル 編

B5判（182 x 257 mm）
上製　箱入り
944ページ（カラー口絵16ページ）
ISBN 4-7700-2130-5

ビジネス、海外駐在、
留学、ホームステイなど、
さまざまな国際交流の場で、
幅広くご活用いただけます。

特色

「日本」を国際的な視点で理解できる幅広い知識と、
実用的な英語が身につきます。

1. 現代の政治制度、最新の経済情報を豊富に記載し、日本を総合的に理解できる。
2. 分野別の構成により、テーマに沿って自然に読み進むことができる。
3. 豊富なイラストと図版を収録し、完全対訳のレイアウトと欄外のキーワードで、重要単語や表現の日英相互参照に便利。
4. 日本国憲法、重要な国際条約、年表をいずれも日英併記で巻末に収録。
5. 英語からも日本語（ローマ字）からも引けるインデックスつき。

内容構成

地理 / 歴史 / 政治 / 経済 / 社会 / 文化 / 生活